BOX 7

BLACK CANYON STAGE ROUTE

Jeanne

Best Wishes,
Susan

Susan and Cricket astride Old Bill

BOX 7
BLACK CANYON STAGE ROUTE

Scratchin' Out a Livin'
on an Arizona Chicken Ranch

by

Susan Harrison McMichael

Illustrations by the Author

All rights reserved. No part of this book shall be reproduced or transmitted in any form or by any means, electronic, mechanical, magnetic, photographic including photocopying, recording or by any information storage and retrieval system, without prior written permission of the publisher. No patent liability is assumed with respect to the use of the information contained herein. Although every precaution has been taken in the preparation of this book, the publisher and author assume no responsibility for errors or omissions. Neither is any liability assumed for damages resulting from the use of the information contained herein.

Copyright © 2010 by Susan Harrison McMichael
Cover Design by R and R Images, Phoenix

ISBN 0-7414-6117-X
Library of Congress Catalog Number 2010937405

Printed in the United States of America

Published September 2010

INFINITY PUBLISHING
1094 New DeHaven Street, Suite 100
West Conshohocken, PA 19428-2713
Toll-free (877) BUY BOOK
Local Phone (610) 941-9999
Fax (610) 941-9959
Info@buybooksontheweb.com
www.buybooksontheweb.com

This book is dedicated to

. . . Mother and Daddy
I wish they were here to set me straight
on some of the details.

. . . my brother, Bill
who was called Cricket in those days

. . . my daughters, Heather, Beth, and Katie
who asked me to tell this story

ACKNOWLEDGMENTS

Writing a memoir is a lonely job, especially when key players in the story are no longer here to help me out. I had to rely on my own memories augmented by bits and pieces of unorganized trivia stuffed into file boxes.

I did have a small cheering section to keep me on track. Heather and Beth rolled up their sleeves and sharpened their pencils. They provided acerbic editorial commentary on preliminary drafts. Katie took it upon herself to be the official photographer of her mother.

Special thanks to Harley Shaw and Jeff McMichael who read the script with shrewd insight. Both are wildlife biologists as well as Arizona historians. Their lives pretty much paralleled mine growing up in post World War II Arizona. They attempted to straighten me out on the flora and fauna of the region as well as links to Arizona history. Any errors I persisted in making are mine alone.

S.H.M.

CONTENTS

Chapter	Page
Preface	1
1. The Black Canyon Trail	3
2. Home to Roost	8
3. A Chicken Ranch! How Come?	13
4. Featherin' the Nest	22
5. Baby Chicks	27
6. F-F-Fonics	31
7. Scratchin' out a Livin'	35
8. Confounded Contraptions	39
9. Are We Poor?	44
10. Denizens of the Desert	49
11. Who Rules the Roost?	55
12. Chicken Soup	58
13. And Not a Drop to Drink	64
14. The Pahlah	70
15. Are We Havin' Fun Yet?	76
16. Old Bill	82
17. Cowboy Cricket	87
18. The Sky Is Falling!	91
19. In Matters Privy	96
20. Chicken on Sunday	103
21. Turkey Trot	107
22. Blank Eggs	111
23. This Little Chick Went to Market	114
24. The Peddler's Wagon	118
25. One of Us	123
26. Saguaro Village	128

27.	Chicken Linen	134
28.	Musicale	137
29.	Zeke the Geek	143
30.	How Does Your Garden Grow?	148
31.	To Bed with the Chickens	153
32.	We'll Kill the Old Red Rooster When They Come	157
33.	She's Flown The Coop	165
34.	Egg-Speriment	169
35.	Golden Cocks	173
36.	Nobody Home But Us Chickens	177
37.	Black-Eyed Peas	184
38.	Chicken Pickin'	188
39.	Box 7, Black Canyon Stage Route	192
40.	The Chicken Or the Egg?	197

ILLUSTRATIONS

	Page
Susan and Cricket astride Old Bill	*Frontispiece*
Daddy! I Have To Go	*5*
The War Years	*19*
Are You Folks Lookin' For a Place To Pick?	*48*
And Not a Drop To Drink	*66*
New Boots	*90*
Family Photos	*101*
Family Photos	*102*
Turkey Trot	*110*
When the Whorehouse Bells Are Ringing	*142*
Wheah Is the Powdah Room?	*163*
I Wonder Why She's Mad?	*196*
The Chicken or the Egg	*198*

PREFACE

The time was immediately after World War II. Mother, a southern belle, and Daddy, a highway department engineer, combined their wartime earnings – Daddy's mustering-out pay from the Navy and Mother's savings from working as a clerk-typist at Fort McClellan, Alabama. In 1946 they threw their lot into the promise of a new life in the form of a desert chicken ranch north of Phoenix. The Ranch was located along the Black Canyon Stage Route, the notorious trail that led adventurers and settlers from Central Arizona (Phoenix) to Prescott and the mountain regions of Arizona.

This memoir spans five years in the life of an intrepid family. Mother and Daddy, neophyte chicken ranchers, struggled through drought, storm, desert vermin, and poultry diseases with grit and humor. Now that I have attained the status of a western matron, I can write about these difficult years with whimsy and a touch of hyperbole.

I figure that a memoir has more latitude than a biography. These tales were witnessed by a little girl from her seventh through her eleventh year. They are my memories and are certainly subject to dispute. I was old enough to be impressionable, and I recall a remarkable amount about our life on this remote homestead. I have been aided by dusty albums, yellowed letters, and even old deeds and receipts. Some of these stories have become part of our family legend. Some tales I have not admitted until now.

The cartoons were part of an album I created for Mother and Dad's 50th Wedding Anniversary in 1986. I hesitated including them in the book because I am not a professional artist. I'm not recognized as a professional author either. So, I shrugged, "What the heck. It's my book. I can put anything in it that I want."

I thought it best to change the names of casual acquaintances. Their identities are unimportant to the story. However, McElroy and John Jacobs were principle farmers in the region. Emma Treadwell was piano teacher to several generations of aspiring musicians, and Velma Teague was long-standing and beloved librarian in the Glendale Public Library. Winnie Ruth Judd, too, was a sensational character in Arizona lore. These names occur as threads within the story.

Our address, Box 7, Black Canyon Stage Route, was a remnant of the Old West. Sixty-five years ago our chicken farm was located in ranch country north of Phoenix. Cultivated crops nurtured by mega-farmers stretched between us and the city. Raw desert, mining claims, and rugged cattle ranches yawned behind us to the county line. Today the Phoenix city limits encompass that land, and red-tiled roofs of housing developments are stacked one upon another.

I thought I'd better capture the memories before they were lost.

Chapter 1
THE BLACK CANYON TRAIL

"Daddy, I gotta go!"

The humpback panel truck shimmied down the gravel trail on bald tires, the result of rationing during World War II. Daddy's white-knuckled hands gripped the steering wheel. He scowled at hairpin curves twisting ahead. The treacherous one-lane passage required concentration and lightning reflexes. As we rounded a blind bend Daddy tapped the horn to assure that another vehicle was not approaching from the upward climb.

"But, Daddy, I gotta go!"

"You'll have to wait," he growled.

"Bad!" I whined.

The brim of Daddy's khaki work hat cocked over his left eye. In profile I could see blue veins throbbing on his temple. A smoldering Camel cigarette dangled from the corner of his mouth creating an acrid haze that permeated the cab of the truck. Daddy was able to inhale the putrid fumes then expel them through his nose in the manner of a smoke stack, all without the use of his hands. When the cigarette was spent to its last inch, Daddy took one hand from the steering wheel, pinched the stub, and added it to a tray full of ashes and butts.

We spiraled down the pock-marked road. The Black Canyon Trail was the primary link between Arizona's central mountain regions to Phoenix and the Valley of the Sun.

"But, Daddy…"

My problem was imminent and pressing. My bladder would not take another bump, and Daddy showed no inclination to stop. Even had he attempted to extricate me from the press of boxes and ropes that held our entourage together, the contrivance was likely to spill willy-nilly over the road. Daddy had figured on a non-stop ride to our destination. The War had kept him away too long, and he did not understand the ways of little girls.

Daddy's exasperation mounted as he assessed the topography. From his side of the truck, a scarred mountain scaled upward, a sheer cut created by blasting caps and hard labor. Precarious stones threatened to tumble on vehicles executing the sharp turns. From my side, a precipice dropped perpendicular from the vehicle. A tipsy guard rail merely suggested defense against plummeting into the abyss. There were precious few places to let a little girl out of the truck to relieve herself.

I crossed my legs and writhed. I was wedged between the truck door and a roll of Navajo rugs. My doll, Agnes, had slipped to the floor and I could not reach her.

I whined again to emphasize my agony. "Daa-Dee!"

We were headed to a new life. Daddy was moving us from temporary lodgings in Flagstaff to a place of our own. Mother followed, steering a 1940 Oldsmobile loaded with clothes and books, pots and pans, plates and platters packed between blankets to prevent breakage. Little brother, Cricket, jostled at Mother's side.

When our caravan rendezvoused at occasional wide spots in the road, Mother appeared riveted to the steering wheel, unable to loose her tense grip on the tool that kept her vehicle from bolting into the sheer gully that outlined the road. Her eyes, wild and catatonic, remained pinned on yet another twist in the trail. Her carefully rouged and lipsticked face at the beginning of the trip was now grey and wan. Her dark hair was powdered with dust that had plumed behind Daddy and me.

Daddy! I Have To Go

We had reclaimed from storage an odd legacy from Daddy's parents – trunks and chairs, bureaus and bedding, washtubs and ironing boards, crystal, what-not, and an upright piano. It was all this that held me hostage in this moment of dire distress.

Daddy was already grouchy when we left Flagstaff mid-morning, hours later than he had planned. Strapping chattel into the vehicles took more time than he had allowed.

So far we had traversed Oak Creek Canyon, noted for its wilderness, its deep canyons, and its trout streams. In the fall of the year this mighty canyon was ablaze with yellow, carmine, and magenta foliage that matched its sculptured walls.

Transitional terrain hosted plant life from both mountain and desert. A few stately ponderosa had migrated from the high country. Spindly piñons nudged between cracks in the boulders. Prickly pear cacti crawled low to the ground in rocky outcrops. An occasional yucca pointed its spears in a radiant arc.

We climbed over sandstone ridges to the small community of Sedona snuggled under protective rocks. The cliffs surrounding Sedona reflected a jeweler's array of burgundy, amethyst, and gold. However, Daddy was not captivated by the brilliance of the scenery. He was a man on a mission. We had miles to go before we stopped.

Our caravan navigated through Grasshopper Flat to the smelter town of Clarkdale. Phelps Dodge Corporation, operating an open-pit mine, extracted copper ore and spewed nasty gases into the atmosphere. We negotiated the winding streets of Jerome, a ghost town whose forsaken homes and businesses clung stubbornly to the sheer sides of Mingus Mountain. We gassed up in Prescott, territorial capital of Arizona until political records had been stolen and deposited in Phoenix.

From Prescott we began the descent via the Black Canyon Stage Route. Since pioneer days miners and missionaries, ranchers and herders, soldiers and settlers, outlaws and sheriffs had traveled this notorious route in search of prosperity and adventure. It might have taken a man and a horse three days to travel the Black Canyon Trail. Daddy optimistically expected to accomplish the same distance in a matter of hours. Mayer (formerly called Big Bug), Cordes, Black Canyon City, Rock Springs were points on the way.

Colorful characters from Arizona history traveled the Black Canyon Trail before us. Bucky O'Neill of Rough Rider fame commandeered a Concord wagon during inclement weather when its drunken driver threw the brake and plunged the conveyance down a steep grade. The coach skittered around curves and bounced over deep chuck holes. O'Neill shoved a heavy six-shooter inside his trouser waistband and clambered to the top of the roiling coach. In an action worthy of a Grade-B western, the hero overwhelmed the errant driver. O'Neill clouted the driver with his pistol, snapped handcuffs onto his wrists, then proceeded to control the stampeding steeds. When the coach came to a halt, O'Neill unceremoniously strapped the driver into the big leather luggage boot behind the stage, dropping him off at the next station to be sent back to Prescott on the next stage north.

It was five decades past the exploits of Bucky O'Neill.

But the road was the same. Graveled, curvy, narrow, steep. The Bradshaw Mountains frowned upon its travelers and dared them to go beyond the next bend. In early days, stage drivers would await each other at turnouts. They carried fog horns and emitted one long blast when they came to a curve. A responding two blasts meant that another wagon was also approaching. If the road was impassable at that juncture, the UP stage gave way to the DOWN stage. In the case of a total impasse the UP team was unhitched, and the coach was rolled back downhill until it reached a point where the two stages could pass.

Automobile drivers over the Black Canyon Trail followed similar protocol. One tap of the horn when approaching a bend. Two taps in response. In the case of a stalemate, courtesy and good sense determined which driver backed off. Fortunately, we did not encounter many vehicles in route.

It was bleak November. Snow had not settled over northern Arizona mountains, but the day was windy and overcast. I drew my coat around me to ward off chill seeping in from cracked windows and rusty floorboards. For a seeming eternity I had been biting my tongue and praying that Daddy find a pullout. Begrudgingly, he finally pulled into a slight widening against the mountain. With decided bad humor, he began to unlace the knot of ropes holding our precarious ensemble together. At last, I was able to relieve myself. I turned my cold little backside to the wind.

Chapter 2

HOME TO ROOST

"Are we there yet?" I whined.

The drive had been interminable, and I had to go to the bathroom again.

"No. This place is called Bumble Bee."

Daddy pointed to a cluster of empty shanties with sagging roofs and doors flapping on rusted hinges.

"A bunch of old prospectors were badly stung when they found a nest of bumble bees in the nearby cliffs as they looked for gold," Daddy told me. "Nobody lives here now."

I didn't know whether to be relieved or vexed. I wanted the trip to end, but the shacks dotting the desert didn't look like tolerable places to live. Mother, certainly, would not have been pleased.

We had gradually transitioned from the pine-studded climatic zone of Northern Arizona to desert expanse. Mother and Cricket bounced gamely behind us, keeping some distance back to avoid eating dust that billowed in our wake.

We were now in cactus country. Legions of giant Saguaros lined the road. Saguaros were the monarchs of the desert. Some stood as tall as fifty feet and had dozens of thorn-laced arms reaching skyward in reverent prayer. As our caravan rolled down the dusty aisle separating rows of congregational Saguaro clusters, we might have been in a colossal cathedral. However, the serious reverence of the situation was lightened by occasional limbs that twisted maniacally about spiked torsos like wild dancers in a discotheque.

Some cacti bristled inhospitably close to the ground. Chollas, linked like spiked sausages, and Prickly Pears, resembling arrangements of thorny pancakes, suggested the makings of an indigestible breakfast.

We slowed down as we passed New River. Daddy said we were on the final leg of our journey. A shady ramada beside the road was a testament to hospitality of the old west. Rusty guns, dusty saddles, whips, and spurs hung from its rafters. New River was an early stage station. A general store was still open for business. We, however, did not stop for its amenities.

The sun was low on the horizon when we turned off the dusty highway onto a narrower and rougher road. A row of mail boxes at the intersection leaned erratically like a line of drunken wranglers. Daddy pulled up to the assemblage.

"That's our box." Daddy pointed to Box 7, sizable and sensible and surprisingly erect, stationed at the end of the line. "Our ranch is one mile down this road."

On the west side of the road, shadows of late afternoon stretched across the hard-packed desert floor. But, when we turned east on the little side road leading to our new home, the miracle of water in the desert was apparent. On one side of the road raw desert was dusty, prickly, and fragile. The opposite side of the road was spread with a carpet of verdant green. Water flowed merrily along straight ditches, and at regular intervals bubbled neatly into cultivated rows of alfalfa. For one mile we straddled the division between parched desert and fertile fields.

And then, on the desert side of the road, a lonely outfit hunkered in the approaching dusk. Daddy slowed when we reached a barbed wire fence that outlined the property. A row of jaunty hollyhocks marched the length of the fence. Someone had a sense of humor when she (of course, it was a woman) planted those giant posies among the tumbleweeds. When we came to a gate Daddy pulled in. The drive from Flagstaff had taken the entire day. We could count on one hand the number

of cars that we encountered along the Black Canyon Trail.
We were home. Home to roost.

Daddy extricated himself from the panel truck. He removed his fedora. The hat band had smashed his hair and left a sweaty indentation around his head. He breathed deeply and ran fingers through his heavy brown mop. Daddy was a little bandy-legged guy, cocky, self-assured. He squared his shoulders and drew himself to his full five-foot-seven frame. He rolled his shoulders and set his hands on his hips. He was poised for the next adventure of his life.

"See that row of buildings, Susie." He pointed to a series of wooden sheds at the back of the property. "We are going to raise chickens in those buildings." Daddy was already calculating the commerce of the land.

Mother and Cricket pulled through the gate. Mother limped out of the dusty Oldsmobile. The harrowing drive had taken its toll on her porcelain prettiness. She was rumpled and mussed. Her face was actually dirty. A layer of silt from the Black Canyon Trail had dusted her nose in place of Cody's translucent powder. Dark tresses had escaped from their bobby-pin confines and strands that were not pasted to her cheeks waved lamely from her coif. Mother wiped a furrowed brow then set *her* hands on *her* hips.

"Where are we going to sleep tonight?" she said.

The Ranch (as we continued to call our ten-acre spread) was empty, abandoned, and sad. It sought a family to rescue it from its loneliness. It needed a business to raise it from its doldrums.

Numerous buildings dotted the spread. They were whitewashed structures with corrugated iron roofs. Two rows of chicken houses (eight in all), a barn, a garage, and even a privy. There were actually two residences on the property, Big House and Little House, and we eventually had occasion to live in each of them.

Daddy had purchased The Ranch for $8750. The $2000 down payment came from his mustering-out pay from the Navy combined with money Mother had saved while she worked at Fort McClellan. Daddy planned to keep his job with the

Highway Department until we were established and The Ranch was paid off. Unfortunately, for now, Daddy's traveling job would take him away from home throughout the week.

Daddy and Mother would put chickens in the eight tidy coops. Mother would throw handfuls of grain to the fowl during the week. And – when Daddy was home on weekends – he would do the other chores.

"All we gotta do is . . ." a favorite phrase of Daddy's.

Our property spanned two sides of the road. Eight acres were on the north side of the road, and two acres were perched catty-cornered, southeast across road. The eight-acre parcel was further segmented. The forward five acres contained all of the buildings. The back three acres was a once-cultivated field bordered by four strands of barbed wire.

The odd parcel across the road was windblown and dusty. It was riddled with earth-hugging prickly pear and menacing cholla. But, the value of that anomalous section lay in the fact that it housed our well which was identified by a galvanized tank teetering atop four spindly wooden stilts. Rusty pocks suggested that it had been the object of target practice by a wayward marksman. From the tank, water was funneled across the road to the troughs and ditches, faucets and hoses, houses and buildings. The success of our operation would hinge on this rusty apparatus and the availability of that water.

Drought-resistant plants provided meager shade. Shaggy tamarisk trees loomed in several undisciplined clusters around the property. They arched above the buildings casting shadows through ungainly thickets of bluish-grey needles. Mesquite trees hunkered near several of the chicken houses. They were low shrubs that harbored razor sharp thorns and dropped drying pods filled with beans.

The only cultivated crop that The Ranch boasted was a row of citrus trees along the east side of the property. Yellow and orange baubles peeked from behind the dark green foliage of lemon, grapefruit, and orange trees. The fruit was just coming into season.

We might have thought we were alone on The Ranch, announcing our arrival only to the haughty saguaros and the wind. But wait, another creature watched us from across the road. A shaggy white head materialized from behind the pump. Two ears twitched apprehensively. Beady black eyes followed us observantly. We must have appeared non-threatening because a little dog trotted across the road to greet us and proceeded to sit on its haunches in a begging manner. I scrambled for some sandwich crusts that were left from our traveling lunch.

"Ugh, where did that scruffy mutt come from?" Mother was still assimilating the prospect of chicken-farming in this barren locale.

This little mutt had fended for herself on gophers and water from a stagnant cow pond since the previous owners had vacated the ranch. Her matted fur was tangled with burrs and bits of tumbleweed. She seemed happy to find companionship and devoured the morsels that I offered.

"What shall we call her?"

Betty Grable was the blonde bombshell of wartime cinema. I likened the dog's motley white fur to Grable's smoothly coifed tresses and dubbed her "Betty." Our new friend rolled gleefully at our feet baptizing herself with desert sand. "Betty" was as good a name as any. She assumed the role of hostess to The Ranch.

Chapter 3
A CHICKEN RANCH! HOW COME?

"A chicken ranch?" Mother gasped.
"Yes, ten acres. All our own!"
"What do we know about raising chickens?"
"We'll learn!"

However, the road to a chicken ranch actually began when a bride went west.

Mother was a mail-order bride (of sorts). She packed a wedding dress, a collection of lace doilies, and a china tea pot, and traveling alone from Alabama, boarded a westbound train.

Daddy met her at Phoenix Union Station with a cast binding his left hand and a wilted rose in his right. Two days earlier, Daddy had accepted a challenge to ride a broom-tailed nag with an uncongenial personality. A five-dollar bet hinged on his staying astride his mount for one minute. The five dollars would contribute to his honeymoon. Daddy bolted out of the chute on Saint Isabella. Twenty seconds into the ride he plummeted under the flailing hooves of the enraged mare. He suffered a broken wrist along with cuts and contusions. If Daddy harbored thoughts of a rodeo career, they were put on hold permanently.

Daddy and Mother had carried on a two-year courtship via United States Mail. Plenty of three-cent stamps were purchased before Mother was convinced to leave the gentle South. Daddy sent money via Western Union for a train ticket west. Mother rolled in on the Union Pacific just in time for the wedding.

"I do." "I do." No family. License signed. Wedded bliss.

Elsie Mae Seale was a southern belle from a family of genteel poverty. Even her name suggested Southern upbringing where double names like Betty Sue, Daisy Lou, and Martha Jean proliferated.

William Johnston (with a "T") Harrison was the son of a prominent Flagstaff family. His father, in the employ of the Forest Service, brought his wife and sons to Flagstaff during pre-statehood days to work at the Coconino Forest Experiment Station (the first USFS research facility established in the nation). Frank Harrison, in time, shed the breeches, boots, and stiff-brimmed hat of the Forest Service and began to dabble in law and politics. He studied independently for the Arizona Bar Exam, passed the test with flying colors, and hung his shingle in Flagstaff. The West was wild. Law was a fledgling enterprise in this lumber, railroad, and ranching center. Legal opportunities abounded concerning matters of gambling, prostitution, bootlegging, cattle rustling, and general hell-raising. By the time Daddy was a young man his father was Judge of the Superior Court of Coconino County.

The Judge wanted his younger son to join the ranks of barristers in Arizona, so Daddy matriculated at the University of Arizona in 1927 and dutifully enrolled in the curriculum required of a lawyer-to-be. Law, however, was not his calling. Half-way through the academic process Daddy left school and drifted into Dixie.

This particular summer the nation lurched to a financial standstill. It was the year of the Crash (1929). The Great Depression was underway. Daddy was lucky to get a job hauling ice in Texarkana, Arkansas. He rattled around town in a wagon toting frozen blocks to meat markets and grocery stores. A year of hefting 100-pound chunks of ice convinced Daddy to return to school.

Instead of returning west, Daddy continued east. He found himself in Alabama. He matriculated U of A again (Alabama this time), enrolled in the College of Engineering, and pursued a degree in the civil side of that persuasion. He graduated in 1934 but not before he met Mother.

Mother graduated high school as the country plunged into Depression. Her father had been a supervisor at a foundry that manufactured conduit used in city drains and in commercial operations. The Depression threw Southern foundries into a tailspin, and her father was reduced to a menial role as a watchman of sorts over the idle leviathan that once employed most of the town. He considered himself lucky to have any job considering what befell most of the workforce.

Mother's memory book suggested that she was a demure young lady who wore her hair bobbed and Marcelled in the mode of the day. She traveled in a popular set of handsome boys and pretty girls. Pressed between the pages of her album were invitations to various social events. The A Club Banquet, "Weston"; The Valentine Dance, "Irby"; 'Bama Theater,"Dick."

After high school Mother talked her way into a job at Zwerling's Shoe Store. She convinced Mr. Z that she was experienced in selling footwear. Mother's strategy was to always say she could do something and then figure out how to do it. Get the job. Ask questions later. She spent two years measuring smelly feet and fitting new shoes on those who could afford them.

The fourth year into the Depression Mother took the bus to Tuscaloosa to visit a cousin. At a get-together of rowdy 'Bama scholars she met an Arizona buck who would soon be graduating with an engineering degree.

They didn't have long to become acquainted. Daddy picked up his diploma, packed his bags, and headed toward the sunset. A long-distance courtship ensued. Two years.

Back in his home town of Flagstaff, Daddy batted around in assorted odd jobs: a courtroom clerk, a tire changer, a service station attendant, a night custodian. He had a hopeful eye on a job with the Arizona Highway Department.

Into the fall a business opportunity arose. Daddy was offered manager-ship of a Texaco enterprise in Ash Fork with the prospect of buying into the franchise. So, he rambled to that lonely railroad town near Route 66 that caught most of its business from visitors headed to the Grand Canyon.

Daddy's endeavor with Texaco in Ash Fork became jaded when a large sign was constructed outside of town. The sign directed traffic toward an alternate route to the Grand Canyon, a route that by-passed businesses in the small community. Business waned in Ash Fork.

Arizona was on the cusp of a new age. Roads and bridges connecting Arizona settlements to one another as well as to the rest of the nation were on the drawing board. When the long-awaited big offer came from the Arizona Highway Department, Daddy wired money for Mother to travel west.

WESTERN UNION

FLAGSTAFF ARIZ   1936 APRIL 15 PM 4 40

TO:
MISS ELSIE SEALE
ANNISTON ALABAMA

SENDING MONEY WESTERN UNION STOP ILL MEET YOU IN PHOENIX

LOVE BILL

Their marriage started upon a continuous detour as Daddy joined a crew that was laying out roads and bridges across a fledgling state. Their peripatetic existence threw Mother and Daddy into rented rooms, line-shacks, and trading posts across The West.

Snippets from Mother's journal and brittle paper fragments tucked between the pages:

Phoenix, Arizona, July 1936
> We're not supposed to be here for long. But why does it have to be in July? The daytime temperature hovers above 110°. Today it registered 113°. At night we trundle out to a sleeping porch where eight cots are lined in a row. It's certainly not honeymoon accommodations! All of the tenants in this

rooming house sleep in the same quarters! It's either that or swelter through the night in our room!

Flagstaff, Arizona, January 1937

I've never been so cold! We left balmy Phoenix after Christmas. Date trees and citrus groves. Flagstaff is experiencing its coldest winter on record! Frozen pillars of ice connect the eaves of the house to the snow piled earth. It is -30°. That is MINUS 30 degrees!

Marble Canyon, Arizona, April 1937

Indians! I cowered in the middle of the bed clutching Bill's rifle across my chest. Three Navajo men milled about outside. They occasionally peeped in the window. In time, the curious savages mounted their shaggy ponies and drifted away. Fortunately, I did not pull the trigger.

Lee's Ferry, Arizona, June 1937

Nothing but a one-room shanty! The floor is riddled with knot holes inviting desert vermin to slither through. No water: we haul it in from the trading post. No electricity: we use a Coleman lantern. Fuel for cooking: we gather cottonwood from the banks of the Colorado River.

Buckskin Mountains, Arizona, January 1938

Buffalo are nothing more than shaggy docile cows. Bill did not have a permit to shoot a buffalo, but we trailed along ostensibly to help with the hunt. I actually walked up to the heard before Sam Jackson and Ralph Hanks shot theirs. Twelve animals were permitted to be killed. The poor beasts didn't have a sporting chance.

Oraibi, Arizona, July 1938

I watched in spellbound horror as masked dancers gyrated in wild supplication for rain. Snakes writhed and coiled around their arms and necks as a chorus of tom-toms throbbed and pulsed. Young boys mesmerized the snakes with feathers attached to sticks to divert the vipers from sinking their venomous fangs into the dancers. And wonder of wonders, following the rain dance, thunderheads gathered over Oraibi.

Fredonia, Arizona, April 1939

A nice lady brought me a loaf of hot bread. She introduced herself as Sister Blakeley. A passel of towheaded children clutched the hem of her skirt. Nestled beside the steaming loaf was a small black volume, *The Book of Mormon*. These people have so many children; I don't see how a man could possibly support more than one family.

Winslow, Arizona, August 1939

'What a shame. But, don't worry, Doctor. We'll keep it anyway.'
That's what Bill said when he saw his new baby girl! He was visibly underwhelmed by the red and wrinkled face and the black-thatched head that tapered to a decided point. Her name is Susan.

Snowflake, Arizona, November 1940

Pig farming! Bill and one of the farmers here entered into a business agreement. Farmer Skousen needed some capital to begin a pork operation. Bill advanced the money for Farmer Skousen to purchase a breeding pair of swine. The loose agreement was that Farmer Skousen would raise the pigs, and when resulting piglets were sold, he and Bill would share the profit. In time a brood of little piggies wriggled about Farmer Skousen's sty. When the piggies went to market Bill approached Farmer Skousen about the profits. Apparently pig farming is not a gainful venture!

Taylor, Arizona, September 1941

Bill is now working for a company called Western Oil. They have road construction contracts across the West. Being named supervisor of this project was a nice advancement in his career.

Alamogordo, New Mexico, 1942

The world is in turmoil. And so are our lives. There is not a vacancy to be had in Alamogordo. The town crawls with military personnel and engineers working at the White Sands Proving Ground. They are perfecting bombs of mass destruction to be used against the Japs and the Krauts. I garnered my pride and went door to door to see if anyone could rent out a spare room. A nice woman, taking pity on my "family way," is letting us stay in her unused bedroom.

Deming, New Mexico, August 1942

Bill says I can name him anything I want as long as he is a junior. So, I recorded William Johnston (with a "T") Harrison,

Jr. on his birth certificate. We are calling the little guy Cricket.

Prescott, Arizona, February 1943

He has a classified job! He should be exempt from active duty! But, Bill says that he couldn't live with himself if he didn't enlist.

Anniston, Alabama, October 1943

Dear Bill,
We are settling in. Mama has put us in a back bedroom. We have tightened our belts and pooled our ration books. I have applied for a job at Ft. McClellan. They need secretaries. I should be able to save a little from each paycheck; then we will have a nest-egg when you come home.

South Pacific, May 1944

Dear Elsie,
Your package arrived today. It takes the mail a long time to catch up with us. When a guy gets a parcel from home he is the envy of all the guys. But, I want you to know that we have candy and cigarettes available on board the ship. So don't send those items. I don't want you to deprive the children. There's not much I can tell you except that we are in the middle of a big dark ocean. Mail is censored.

The War Years

Susan Harrison McMichael

Anniston, Alabama, November 1944
Dear Bill,
I am overcome with guilt. All of our ration coupons for shoes have been spent keeping the children shod. They out-grow shoes before they out-wear them. I'm saving Susie's shoes for Cricket, but as yet, he is too small to wear her hand-me-downs. And, I haven't had a new pair of shoes since we were married. Through a friend of a friend of a friend I learned of a man who had a closet full of ladies' shoes for sale. I called the number that I was given, and he agreed to meet me. I expected the exchange to occur in a dark alley. He, however, invited me to his home. He showed me a modest selection of shoes. I chose a pair of sensible black pumps, paid him an outrageous $7, and slipped away with my Black Market purchase.

South Pacific, 1945
The end of The War was imminent. A massive invasion of the Imperial Empire was being planned under wraps of greatest secrecy. Daddy's ship was scheduled to be part of a big push to topple Japan. Before the invasion by sea transpired, the U.S. sent bombers laden with massive atomic weapons to Hiroshima and Nagasaki. Japan surrendered in short order.

Daddy came home.

En route to Flagstaff, Arizona, 1945
"We'll get back in time for Susan to start school."

We trundled through southern Arkansas and started across a vast expanse called Texas.

Daddy yodeled, "The sun is riz, the sun is set. Here we is, in Texas yet!"

Three days across Texas and New Mexico and we finally chugged over the Arizona border. Daddy chortled a parody of the California theme song: "Arizona, here we come! Right back where we started from! Open up them Corral Gates. Arizona, here we come!"

I was ready to begin first grade. Cricket was three years old. We settled in post-war housing in Flagstaff while Daddy regained his land legs. He returned to a job with the Arizona Highway Department as an engineer who inspected a flurry of highway construction projects that had been put on hold for the duration of The War. But, Daddy wanted something other than a government job. His stint in the Navy solidified his loathing for bureaucracies. He would salute no man. Daddy was an adventurer, a speculator, a pioneer. Within the year Daddy came home with an announcement.

"A chicken ranch! Near Phoenix."

Chapter 4

FEATHERIN' THE NEST

When we first moved to The Ranch we took up residence in the larger house. Big House was a boxy frame structure with a screen porch across the kitchen side and a steep corrugated iron roof. We had to walk up several steps to reach the level of the porch. Perhaps when we were getting settled Big House was more readily habitable. Big House had been built as a single square room. Across one end plumbing was installed, and a kitchen and a bathroom were scabbed in. The big room was divided in half by a lath wall. One side was the kitchen/living room. The other side was the bedroom/bathroom. Mother further subdivided the bedroom with a curtain made from an old bedspread, Mother and Daddy's side and children's side.

Big House had probably been the primary residence on The Ranch. An attempt at landscaping was apparent. Two mature eucalyptus trees shaded the west side of the house. At the foot of the steps, leading to what we called the front door, a pathetic flower garden was outlined by a row of desert rocks. The soil had been tilled so that it was softer than the ground around it, but this simply encouraged the invasion of ragged weeds. In fact, a robust tumbleweed had taken root. It looked like the skeleton of a spiny shrub. On the next windy day the tumbleweed would break from its roots and begin a rollicking journey over the desert floor.

The last trace of a woman's touch around the house was evident in the form of a climbing rose bush. A single spindly stalk clung tenaciously to a small trellis nailed to the house. Its leaves were sparse, and a lonely red rose unfolded at the top of the vine.

Cricket and I were wild with delight at the prospect of horses and cattle, cowboys and Indians, bunkhouses and chuck wagons, those images we saw on Saturday matinees featuring Roy Rogers and Gene Autry. We hadn't yet grasped that on this ranch we would be wrangling chickens. We shed our overcoats and galoshes and played in shirt sleeves under the citrus trees. We pulled oranges and gorged on sweet pulp as sticky juice ran down our chins and elbows. We frolicked with Betty. The abandoned dog made her way into our hearts. Neighbors told us that the previous owners had not been able to find Betty after their wagon was packed and they were ready to pull out of the yard.

"I'll bet Betty stayed here just for us," I exclaimed.

Betty accompanied Mother and Daddy as they assessed The Ranch. She trotted along with me when I dashed to the gate to catch the bus to my new school. When the same bus deposited me at the gate at the end of the day, Betty romped over to greet me. When coyotes howled in the distance Betty joined the chorus. She barked vigilantly when an occasional truck rattled down the road. All in all, Betty took very seriously the task of custodian to our new home.

Our first few weeks at The Ranch were spent in a flurry of getting chicken coops ready for the first brood. Little was done about getting our own living quarters ready for habitation.

"Time for that later," Daddy said.

We lived out of crates and boxes. Christmas approached, and an unsettled holiday loomed. Daddy brought a scraggly piñon tree in from his week on the highways up north. We decorated it with hand-crayoned paper ornaments that I crafted at school. Big House took on an air of humble festivity.

It was the day before Christmas.

"Oh, no!" I fretted. "I want to make a Christmas present. A Christmas present for Mother and Daddy."

Gift resources on the ranch were sparse. I let myself into the building that we called the garage, identified such by double plank doors wide enough to admit a tractor or a hay wagon, but crammed so full of claptrap that its intended purpose was lost. The garage was stacked with unpacked boxes destined for the house. It also contained rabble left by the former tenants. Snaggle-toothed rakes and cracked hoses, tangles of barbed wire, stacks of citrus boxes in various states of wholeness, hard and splayed paintbrushes, rusty-dusty objects of dubious use. In the dim light I saw a shelf of paint cans. I explored. Most were sealed with desiccated layers of crust. I shook a small can that claimed to contain red paint. There seemed to be fluid in the can. I pried the lid off with a pointy utensil, and sure enough, there was a small portion of viscous red substance in the can. I knocked around the citrus boxes and found one that had four sides and a bottom.

"What can I make with this?" I lamented.

I could paint the box. But what would it be? I would make a bookcase – books already littered the flat surfaces in our house. With fervor I tackled my project envisioning something useful for our home. I procured a stiff paintbrush and smeared red goo over the rough boards. My hands and arms, as well as my ragged overalls, consumed a good portion of the paint. I covered most of the box with virulent color. The inside had to go unpainted because I expended the contents of the paint can over the side boards and the back. I left my project amid dusty clutter to dry.

Later in the day, I returned to wrap my gift, but alas, the Sunday comics that I had purloined from the kitchen table were neither large enough nor strong enough to encompass my gift. I ran back to the kitchen and robbed Mother's cupboard of two large dish towels to swath the present. I held the towels together with safety pins. The resultant package was like a badly secured diaper. Sadly, the paint was not fully dry, so the towels stuck to the surface of the box. It was this rough object reeking of paint fumes that I placed under the Christmas tree.

"Do you think Santa will find us this year?" I worried.

"I imagine so. You left a map for him didn't you?"

Mother tucked Cricket and me under the covers early on Christmas Eve.

"Yes, but we left the map beside the cookies. Santa is going to need the map to find the cookies."

My faith in Santa was tempered for another year. Cricket and I had tacked limp stockings to the window ledge because a classic fireplace mantle was absent from Big House. When we upended the socks on Christmas morning, apples, nuts, and hard candies rolled over the floor. The prize was a shiny nickel in the toe of each sock. Santa left customary gifts for children under the tree. I discovered a doll, a game, and a book. And Cricket discovered comparable boy toys.

I watched apprehensively as Mother and Daddy peeled dishtowels from my humble offering. Mother burst into tears.

"Oh, Mother," I lamented. "I'm sorry I ruined your dish towels."

Mother carefully pulled the sticky box away from the sweaters and slippers and books and toys that were piled in disarray under the tree.

"This is the perfect shelf for our *Reader's Digests*," she assured me. "It will go in the bedroom." And it did. Next to the wall. Under the bed. A receptacle for old magazines.

Just because it was Christmas Day did not mean that there wasn't work to do.

"First, let me get the turkey in the oven. Then I'll go out with you." Mother was talking to Daddy.

Mother set the big bird to bake and accompanied Daddy to examine the condition of a chicken house where Daddy planned to put his first batch of chicks to be ordered after the New Year.

At the corner of the outbuilding, a scrubby mesquite provided a lacy den, and on this chilly Christmas morning, a safeguard from the elements. Odd whimpering and mewling sounds came from the thicket. I looked down. There was a hole in the ground created by a dislodged rock. It was about four inches square and about six inches deep. A white tail, the size of a little finger, flicked helplessly.

"It's a puppy!" I squealed.

A baby puppy was stuck head-first in the hole. Only his tail was free to signal his distress. Betty, as mangy as ever, was snuggled under the canopy. Four puppies vied contentedly for her teats. Betty had been placidly ignoring her distressed pup. However, she nuzzled it fondly when I placed him among his siblings. This was the best of all presents from Santa.

Chapter 5
BABY CHICKS

"Aren't they dear?" Mother scooped a fluffy white chick into the palm of her hand. This endeavor might actually be fun. Nonetheless, Mother developed a love-hate relationship with the chickens shortly after the first boxes arrived from the hatchery. We drove to Glendale to retrieve five cardboard cartons stacked in a corner at the hatchery. An occasional head popped through air holes in the heavy cardboard cartons, and cottony puffs gibbered like quarreling brats.

Daddy grunted, "These will go in the east coop." But I could tell that he was proud, ready to begin his new enterprise.

Back-breaking preparation had gone into the arrival of this first batch of chicks. Their new home was cleaner than Mother's kitchen. Mother and Daddy had scrubbed the coop from floor to rafters with Lysol to rid the enclosure of lurking germs that might bring on an outbreak of brooder pneumonia, fowl pox, bumblefoot, or breast blisters – all warned of in literature my parents had consumed about chicken farming. Chickens were subject to a litany of ominous poultry diseases that went on to include Coccidiosis, Mareks Disease, Omphalitis, Newcastle Disease, and Infectious Coryza. Not only did their habitat have to be meticulously clean, chickens themselves had to be regularly medicated through immunization drops in their water. These babes twittered blissfully unaware of the multitude of lurking maladies.

Their home had become a sturdy white-washed building, 15 feet by 15 feet, wood lath the lower half and wire netting the upper half. It was capped by a corrugated iron roof. When the chicks were bigger and worldlier, a trap door along the bottom of one wall would be raised, and the chicks would be allowed into a fenced side-yard where they could scratch for grubs and worms.

Like human infants, chicks had to be nurtured through a transitional phase. It was the dead of winter, early in January. Admittedly, winter in southern Arizona was not wrought with the icy fury of northern latitudes. Days were generally balmy, sweater weather. But, night on the desert could be downright chilly. Little chicks had to be kept warm.

The center of the coop was prepared for them. A brooder lamp hung from an electric outlet overhead. It provided warmth through the frosty nights. Under the lamp were several metal trough feeders that contained a sprinkling of mash, nourishment appropriate for the newbies. Sawdust was spread about to provide a layer of insulation from the hard and cold concrete.

One by one Mother discharged her new babies from the crates onto the cement floor. Never again did little chicks that came for temporary asylum at The Ranch receive such decorous pampering. The chicks drew together like magnets and chattered in confusion. Five hundred cotton balls moved as one undulating blanket.

The chicks needed water. Water founts stood like a row of galvanized top hats. The lids could be removed and water poured into the cans. Water then trickled into shallow trays made especially for chicks.

The chicks were incredibly stupid. We had to teach them to drink. We lifted numerous tufts of soft down and dipped their beaks into the water. The rest were supposed to learn by example. Instead, the vicious creatures jostled and shoved and proceeded to try to drown one another.

Daddy got us started. The building was clean. The chicks were settled. Sacks of mash were stacked in the barn. We were ready to watch the chickens grow. On Monday morning Daddy went on the road.

"All you gotta do is keep them fed and watered." Daddy waved and returned to his other job, building highways that lured restless Easterners to the up-and-coming state of Arizona.

Mother might have assumed that since the chickies had a home she could put her energies into settling our house. She was still digging through suitcases to find socks for me to wear to school. But, her new brood required as much care as her old one. She was up before the sun. Set coffee to perk on the butane range. Out to the brooder house. Removed brainless birds that drowned in shallow water troughs. Incinerated them. Back to the kitchen to make oatmeal. Out to the brooder house. Filled water founts. Back to the kitchen to stir the oatmeal and rouse sleepy children. Out to the brooder house. Filled the mash trays. Back to the kitchen to urge a dawdling Susie to get her things together to catch the school bus. Out to the brooder house. Rescued birds that fell victim to bullies beaks. Isolated them. Back to the kitchen to wipe Cricket's oatmeal-smeared face. Threw dishes in the sink. Back to the brooder house. Swept the floor and spread fresh sawdust. And so it went . . .

The chicks moved in a suffocating mass. The weak were trampled and extinguished. The tight knot of chicks loosened during the day. They found their water. They found their food. But, at night they joined ranks again as a thick blanket.

One frosty morning I went with Mother to check the chickies. They were bigger now, more confident. At this insolent adolescent stage they still bore ragged remnants of downy fuzz. The group was in its usual circular mass under the brooder lamp. Most of the birds were asleep. A few complacent peeps suggested their drowsy comfort. Their heads were down, their little rumps up, like chenille bumps. The white blanket rippled and surged, soft and inviting as a cloud. In the middle of the gathering a familiar white stalk flicked and waved. It was out of sync with the chicks' rumps.

Our entrance brought the brood to life. Fresh water and fresh food was on the way. Like a dandelion puff, the mass dispersed. When the cozy coverlet dissolved, Betty's runt Christmas puppy was exposed. He whimpered and mewled.

His cover was lifted. The little guy who started his life in a lonely hole sought warmth and comfort in the brooder house among the chicks. The chicks had harbored him through the chilly night.

Cricket had taken to calling the puppy Tiger.

"Ah," chuckled Mother, "We have a Tiger in chicks clothing."

Chapter 6
F-F-FONICS

"I didn't learn anything that I didn't already know!" I pouted when Mother met the school bus at the gate after my first day at New School. I didn't see any point in continuing my education. It was much more fun to explore our new environs.

New Teacher had assigned me to a squatty chair at a little square table. Among my table mates was a swarthy lad with a shock of stringy black hair that drooped over his eyes. He must have given lip-service to a comb because his front locks still bore damp ridges left by comb teeth, but his back hair bristled like porcupine quills. Although his face gleamed from serious scrubbing, I could see a ring of dirt around his neck. Like many second graders, some of his teeth were missing, and new incisors were beginning to emerge giving him the appearance of a gopher.

New Teacher introduced me to "Hay-soose." His name, according to the tent sign sitting in front of him, was "Jesus." After I could read better I took issue with the way he spelled his name. Besides, who would name a kid Jesus?

A stodgy grey stucco building, Washington School stood sentry at a juncture of two unpaved roads, far outside the Phoenix city limits, Northern Avenue and Mission Drive. Central cement steps lead to a hallway of doors studded with frosty-paned windows. The doors at the top of the stairs were identified as administrative offices, the principal and the nurse.

Other doors wrapped around the u-shaped formation were simply numbered one through eight.

First grade through eighth grade, students progressed through these hallowed halls. Creaky oak floors gleamed dully from daily doses of oiled sawdust and industrial mops. Black slate boards bore assignments of the day from simple ABC's to algebraic equations. Voices murmured behind closed doors. Scholars recited their facts. Teachers scolded.

I stepped into the routine of Washington School. Every day, when first-bell rang, my class gathered at the foot of the front steps. We formed two military lines, boys and girls, and when second-bell rang we marched behind Teacher into our room. The ritual never varied. With roll book in hand, Teacher peered over her spectacles to check the attendance. If anyone was absent she scribbled a name on a piece of paper and attached it to a clip at the door. After attendance records were dispatched, Teacher told the class to rise for the Pledge of Allegiance.

Chairs scraped across the polished oak planks; one tottered backwards and crashed to the floor. Books slammed. A few papers fluttered wildly and came to rest under a table. Teacher frowned. The solemnity of the occasion was compromised.

We took turns leading The Pledge of Allegiance. Teacher posted a chart on the bulletin board, and unless a student had been a complete miscreant he lead the pledge when his name was next on the list.

After a few weeks it came my turn to pay homage to the flag. The Stars and Stripes draped languidly from a post to the left of the blackboard. I took the leader's position at the front of the class. I faced the flag and placed my hand over my heart. With dignity and clarity I pronounced words intended to pay respect to the emblem of our nation.

I led a pigeon to the flag
Of the United States of America
And to the public
Where witches dance

Box 7, Black Canyon Stage Route

One *Asian*
Invisible
With *liver tea*
And *just us*
For all.

For the duration of my school days a 48-star flag hung at the front of every classroom. Since that day that I mangled our country's oath, two words have been added to the pledge, and two stars have been added to the banner.

A free-standing building behind Washington School was the bathroom. Girls on the west side, boys on the east side. The janitors scoured it daily with copious doses of Clorox, but the overriding fragrance was of body odor and urine. Shortly into the day sinks were scummy. Certain toilets did not flush properly. The doors to the stalls were etched with words beyond my comprehension. Big girls stood in front of cracked mirrors, combed their hair, and smeared lipstick over their lips as well as over the reflective glass. A lot of derisive giggling took place in the girls' bathroom.

My classroom learning in Flagstaff transferred to my new school. Primary students of the day learned to read via the Dick and Jane books. "This is Dick. This is Jane. See Dick run. See Jane run. Run Dick run. Run Jane run."

Dreary. But an entire generation learned to read as Dick and Jane and their pets, Spot and Puff, capered over the pages. New words, incessantly repeated, were introduced to the curriculum.

"This is a duck. Duck says quack. Duck. Duck. Quack. Quack. Quack duck quack."

Until now, my reading abilities were confined to words that I read on the Dick and Jane pages. I regurgitated them. My "ah-HA" moment of reading occurred in the girls' bathroom. My reading awareness transferred to words beyond the Dick and Jane books. Scrawled across the mirror in red lipstick was a word remarkably like *duck*. By changing the first sound I had a new word in my reading vocabulary.

I literally danced off the school bus that afternoon to

enlighten Mother about my progress in reading.

As quickly as I had added a new word to my vocabulary, I was instructed to delete it.

Chapter 7
SCRATCHIN' OUT A LIVIN'

Boxes of little chicks arrived every five weeks. They were installed in sterile facilities, pampered like newborn babies, and raised through the truculent teens. Each rotation started out with 500 hatchlings. Mother and Daddy divided the lot in half and placed 250 chicks in each of two houses. There they were warmed, coddled, fed, watered, and entertained.

I suppose Mother was glad that Daddy had elected to begin a chicken enterprise instead of a pig farm. Daddy managed to convince her that chickens had to be easier to manage than cloven-hoofed livestock.

"Pigs!" Mother groaned. She recalled that Daddy had, after all, invested in an unsuccessful pig operation years earlier. At least in that enterprise she was not involved in slopping the hogs.

But, raising chickens involved more than tossing out a few handfuls of grain to them each day. The key to a successful chicken-raising venture was to think like a chicken.

Our chicks were products of a deprived environment from the start. They were hatchery bred. They did not have a mother hen to raise them, to protect them, to lead them to feed and water, in general, to see that they were well-adjusted. Mother filled the role of Little Red Hen in their lives. She talked to them, even sang to them, as she moved among them, trying carefully not to crush one underfoot.

Raising chickens was a seven-day-a-week job. Mother didn't even think of sitting down to her morning coffee before making a circuit of the chicken houses. Although chickens thrived in clean quarters, they did nothing to contribute to their tidiness. Chickens scattered their food, spilled their water, left their droppings in the water fonts, and proceeded to cannibalize one another. From the break of day Mother measured food, wiped water spills, scoured water founts, removed dead birds.

"Ah! And to think I detested ordinary housekeeping," Mother lamented.

Early-on our chicks established a pecking order. Had they been part of a multi-generational family, older birds would have naturally dominated younger birds (and rightly so). But our single-generation flocks encouraged chicks to contend among themselves for supremacy. Birds that were low in peck order were chased away from feeders and watering troughs.

"When Susie and Cricket squabble, I can, at least, send them to opposite corners of the room before bloodshed begins." Mother picked up a wretched chick cowering and bleeding in the corner of the coop and set him in an isolation cage.

Our chickens would eat almost anything. They filled their gizzards with small stones which helped them digest rotten fruit, wilted lettuce, stale bread, eggshells, bugs, worms, grubs, termites. Mother tempered this gross diet with prescribed portions of nutrition-enhanced meals.

"Come and get it!" Mother called needlessly as she poured grain into their food troughs. The chickens were already jostling around her feet.

Chickens required sand, sun, and fun. Our chickens had requisite doses of those ingredients. Their sense of fun included preening, head-scratching, and mutual grooming. When they were bigger and permitted to move freely between chicken coop and side yard we'd often see a chicken flapping about in a small basin of dust. He looked as if he had gone amok. Then, as instantly as he began his bizarre tirade, he flopped, spread-eagle, in the dirt as if dead. Soon he would hop up, ruffle his feathers and strut away from his pleasurable sand bath.

Raising chickens was a business. Records. Records.

Records. Mother was supposed to keep track of feed prices, portions, equipment expenses, antibiotics, and sales. There was a special column in her ledger for mortalities. Here, she was to document how each dead bird met its demise. In her general busy-ness, often weeks would pass, and Mother would not have made a single entry.

Daddy sighed dismally as he thumbed through the empty pages. "How can we correct the problems if we don't know how the birds died?"

"They egg-spired," was Mother's weary retort.

Our commercial enterprise revolved around raising and selling White Leghorn pullets. Although pullet is by definition a female chicken, the term was generally used to describe any young, meat chicken. By ten weeks of age they were of a desirable size to send to market. We also raised to maturity a dozen or so Rhode Island Red hens simply for their eggs. The six or eight eggs a day that they produced during key laying season kept our family in a plethora of eggs and allowed Mother to sell an occasional dozen to farm laborers who stopped by, asking for *huevos*.

At the prescribed time the Leghorns were sent to a slaughter house. A big stake-bed truck loaded with wire cages wheeled through the gate. It pulled up next to a coop of chickens destined for market, and the rodeo began. Herding chickens was somewhat akin to herding cats. They dodged, flapped and scattered six directions as Mother and Poultry Broker chased frantic birds into cages set strategically at trap doors located on the sides of the buildings. Ultimately they were destined for grocery stores and restaurants around Phoenix.

Poultry Broker pulled a zippered bank bag from inside his vest and began peeling off crisp bills to Mother. It looked like a fortune. When Cricket saw the thick stack of greenbacks accumulating in Mother's hands he whooped and danced, "We're rich! Hooray! We're rich!"

As it turned out, one dispatch of pullets to market did not make us rich. That money was immediately channeled into another flock taking up residence in another coop. Or into fixing the house.

* * *

When we moved to The Ranch, Daddy's plan had been to enhance Big House. The interior needed refining. The exterior needed a spruce-up. Rather than paint the rough wooden boards that comprised the sides of the house Daddy decided to stucco. Stucco would give the house a much-needed face lift. It would conceal irregularities in construction and give the structure a pleasing uniform appearance.

Mother learned more than she ever wanted to know about remodeling. The stuccoing job occurred over a series of weekends. Daddy did the hard part, but Mother was right under the ladder handing him tools and brads, pieces of lath, and rolls of wire mesh as they stretched a foundation for the stucco.

"Oh! Just look at my hands!" Mother examined her chafed and cracked fingers. Her formerly manicured nails were ragged and rimmed with grime.

More weekends followed. The operation of a chicken ranch did not stop because Mother and Daddy were stuccoing a house. A flock of pullets went to market, and their coop had to be scrubbed and sterilized. A round of new chicks became sickly, and the entire bunch had to be incinerated. Further cleaning and sterilization. Cantankerous Well across the road was finicky. Daddy tinkered with the cams and rods, belts and pulleys that urged water to our land.

Covering the lath and wire base over the house was a three-coat process – a scratch coat, a grey coat, and a white finish coat. It was like icing a birthday cake three times over. Patch by patch, Mother and Daddy troweled the putty-like stucco over the walls of the house.

The result was a white dove in the desert. A trim tidy residence. At last we were going to settle in.

Chapter 8
CONFOUNDED CONTRAPTIONS

"He'd better not die and leave me on these Godforsaken acres!" Mother marched out to the chicken coops and flung grain to the ungrateful fowl.

Bell Telephone had not stretched wires along our road. A payphone in Glendale, fifteen miles away, was our closest facility for distance communication. By the time we drove there Mother or Daddy could already have achieved any manner of personal contact – ordered items from the feed and seed store, made a doctor's appointment, or arranged for butane delivery.

Daddy could not call when he was delayed on a construction project and would not get home on a Friday night. Mother went through great anguish hoping that Daddy had not run his panel highway truck off the embankment of an unimproved road. She wavered between tragic concern for Daddy's well-being and helpless rage at being so isolated.

"The 20th Century has certainly not reached this part of Arizona," Mother bewailed.

That was not completely true. Certain advancements of the modern age had crawled out from civilization and made life somewhat bearable in the desert. For instance, electric power lines draped from pole to pole along lonely country roads. In fact, an electric sub-station was but a few miles from our ranch. So, our house and all of the auxiliary buildings were electrified.

We read by dim light bulbs that dangled from frayed wires suspended from the ceiling. We tuned in to *Our Miss Brooks* on the radio. And, in the heat of summer, electricity ran a "swamp cooler" hanging outside of the front window. It pulled hot air through wet excelsior pads where it was cooled by evaporation, then circulated through the house by a rattley fan. The humid breeze created a degree of comfort in the house. Electricity also activated the pump that drew water from Cantankerous Well across the road. Thus, we had running water and a flush toilet contingent upon its vagaries.

Daily life was comprised of a series of disparate possessions and customs. We ate our meals off of chipped crockery, but sipped our orange juice from Waterford tumblers. Dinner was set on a faded oilcloth table cover, but we wiped our lips with damask napkins. A rich mahogany mantel clock chimed the hours atop a splintery citrus crate. A globe of the world occupied a niche in the corner, nations suspended in time by pre World War I boundaries.

Antediluvian devices employed to keep us clean and fed might have been snatched from a house of horrors. Mother cooked on Butane Stove, a recalcitrant creature that wheezed and spit and finally ignited in flaming tongues when Mother timidly stuck a match to its burners. Oven and broiler alike needed matches to trigger their operation. At arms length, Mother held a burning match over a small hole in the gas pipe. With her free hand, she reached for the gas dial. Simultaneously, she closed her eyes and turned the gas valve ON. Moments passed; gas hissed. WHOOSH! And an inferno leapt forth. Singed eyebrows gave Mother a perpetually amazed expression. Only two of stove's burners worked with a modicum of efficiency, and even they shot irregular flames along the base of Mother's skillets. One side of a pancake would be scorched while the other side wept oozing batter.

We had a positively medieval electric toaster that guaranteed we would eat burned toast every morning of the week. The inner wires of the contraption were exposed and shot treacherous sparks when the apparatus was plugged into a wall socket. Two pieces of breakfast bread were placed on racks on opposite sides of the toaster. Then, the racks were lifted allowing one side of each slice of bread to be scorched by sparking coils. Before the toast started to burn, we were supposed to release the sides of the toaster and turn the bread so that its undone side would get a chance at electrocution. We often missed this critical turn leaving one side of the bread burned and hot, the other side burned and cold.

"Yum, yum, this is just like toast is 'sposed to be." Daddy scraped his charred offering. "It just needs a little bit of that peach jam."

Mother washed clothes in an antiquated Kenmore "Water Witch." It resembled an oil drum on stilts. A gruesome agitator ratcheted back and forth drawing socks and pillow cases into a netherworld of vicious mechanisms. We might as well have fed our clothes to a bulldog.

On wash day Mother piled mountains of dirty clothes under the awning of a lean-to shed – dainties and whites, sheets and towels, dresses and shirts, Levis and overalls. She would then set a big kettle on Butane Stove and with a pan of water and a box of Faultless Starch concoct a gruel that looked like flour paste. She pushed it to the back of the stove for later use.

Mother set two galvanized wash tubs on a bench. Water Witch loomed beside them casting a malevolent spell. Mother filled the three tubs with water from the garden hose. But, not before she was sure that water from Cantankerous Well was flowing clean and clear.

Water Witch's hard rubber wringers rotated so that clothes, after being agitated in the barrel, were squeezed between them to tub #1 for the first rinse. The wringer rollers were a hazard, grabbing fingers along with ragged towels being sent to the next barrel. When the emergency lever was slammed to rescue smashed fingers, a lethal jaw snapped up and out decking anything in its arc. Nose, chin, and teeth were preferred targets.

The wringers rotated again, and clothes were sent to tub #2 for the second rinse. They rotated again, and the "wrung" clothes were dropped into a wicker basket to be hung on the clothes line or draped over the fence. At this point, shirts and school dresses and Daddy's khaki trousers went through yet another step and were dipped in the goopy Faultless Starch mixture waiting on the stove. When the garments were pinned to the line they dried like cardboard cutouts.

On ironing day Mother employed Sad Iron. Sad irons were actually devices that early pioneers had used to groom their clothes. They were cast-iron, boat-shaped weights heated on a fireplace and rotated one with another. The "weary warsher woman" used one iron to smooth her clothes and then the other as the first reheated.

Mother's iron was actually electrified. But it was a torturous device, void of heat control and steaming systems. Etymologically the *sad* in sad iron (or *sadiron*) was an old word for solid. Mother wasn't interested in the etymology of the word. Sad Iron was perfectly appropriate because ironing was a depressing task.

On wash day, dry laundry was unpinned from the line, folded, stacked, and put away in drawers or on shelves, but on ironing day, Mother was confronted with a basket stuffed with garments that had to be properly smoothed and sharply creased. Mother "sprinkled" these clothes to get them damp enough that Sad Iron would glide across the fabric. I thought re-moistening the clothes was a redundant exercise because, just yesterday, we had gone to great lengths to get the clothes dry. Why couldn't they go straight from rinse tub to "ironing board," a plank Mother set across the backs of two chairs and padded with old towels? She set about to smooth garments that would immediately be snatched off the hangers, worn, soiled, and tossed in a hamper only to go through the cycle again. By the end of ironing morning the house smelled like a Chinese laundry and felt like a sweat lodge. A row of freshly ironed shirts and dungarees, blouses and dresses, napkins and pillow cases, hung from clothes hangers hooked over a pipe rod.

"Don't touch that shirt!" Mother yelped. She hurled herself in front of the rack of newly ironed clothes as Daddy reached for yet another clean shirt.

Our pre-War Oldsmobile sedan took a beating by hauling bags of feed, bales of hay, fence posts, barbed wire, and cartons of chicks. In time, we acquired a Model A Pickup Truck (twenty years beyond its prime) to do that work. It hiccupped and coughed during its tenure and finally came to rest on splayed tires. Eventually, Daddy bought a new and proper ranch wagon, a 1948 Chevy Pickup. But, that was later.

The core to survival on The Ranch hinged on Cantankerous Well. Every morning Mother or Daddy threw a switch that set off a series of convolutions. The pump went into action. A giant gear began to rotate. The large gear was linked to a smaller gear by a heavy rubber belt. The gears screeched in protest; finally in unison, they started to turn. They ground slowly at first, and the pump that plunged rods into the bowels of the earth began pulsing. Faster and faster the gears turned. Steadier and steadier the pump achieved a solid rhythm. Water was drawn up to a galvanized tank perched on tall risers. When the tank was filled, we parsimoniously distributed water across the road. We irrigated citrus trees. We filled water troughs. We washed clothes and dishes. We took our showers. We moistened our parched lips.

Chapter 9
ARE WE POOR?

"Can I get a strawberry shake?" I implored. But I already knew the answer.

"We'll just order small cones today."

Mother, Cricket, and I were sitting at the counter at Upton's Ice Cream Parlor.

"A strawberry cone," I growled ungraciously when the waitress appeared to take our orders.

"Mother, are we poor?" I continued.

Mother answered, "Poor is a state of mind."

At night when I was abed I could hear Mother and Daddy in the kitchen.

"... and $49 for the mortgage," Daddy muttered.

"Bill, I have to order butane. The tank is almost empty," Mother contributed.

"Butane," Daddy added that to his list.

... and mash for the new chicks, grain supplement for the pullets, ground oyster shells for the laying hens...

"Dr. Johnson's bill came yesterday," Mother added.

When the bills were paid Mother stretched what we had left to buy coffee (85¢/ 2# can), flour (40¢/ 10# bag), soup (8¢/ can), bread (13¢/ loaf), salt (10¢/ box), soap powder (29¢/ box), shortening (68¢/ 3# can). Medicine and toiletries came out of the same budget: hand lotion (79¢/ bottle), tooth paste (47¢/ tube), bath soap (8¢/ bar), and aspirin (39¢ / bottle).

There was always a lot of month left at the end of the money.

If I had a nickel in my pocket when we went to town, I indulged in special treats. I could get a bottle of Coca Cola from the grocer's refrigerator chest. Or a single dip strawberry cone at the fountain. Or a Hershey bar with almonds at the candy counter. I needed a dime if I were to splurge on a *Felix the Cat* comic book.

Every Monday morning Mother put a quarter in my pocket. This was milk money. I could have taken five cents a day, but Mother preferred to pay for it by the week. Teacher collected milk money, and every day at lunchtime she gave me a miniature bottle of milk processed by Westward Ho Dairy. These half-pint glass bottles were diminutives of the quarts sold at the grocery store.

The little round cardboard caps we pulled off the tops of the bottles served another function. Teacher had us save the caps, and after lunch she gave lessons in telling time. We sat at our tables and drew clock faces on the little milk bottle tops, then added a small hour hand and a longer minute hand to the time that Teacher instructed.

One Monday morning I did not have my quarter when I arrived at school.

"You can bring it tomorrow, Susan," Teacher consoled me.

"But, Mother gave it to me," I wailed.

"We will give you milk today. Maybe you will find your quarter."

I returned home in bad humor. I had not found my quarter. I had to tell Mother that I needed another quarter for milk money.

Mother said, "You'll have to ask your Daddy."

And, I fretted until Daddy came home.

The sun was setting when Daddy pulled in the gate. I met him with my tale of woe.

He pursed his lips and drew his eyebrows into stern commas over the bridge of his nose. He reached into his pocket, pulled out a few coins, and selected a quarter.

"I found this by the gate when I drove in. You'd better be

more careful from now on." Daddy handed me the coin.

I accepted the coin gratefully. I truly believed that in the waning light and from his perch high in a paneled wagon that Daddy had spotted my lost quarter.

If we weren't poor, we were certainly frugal. *Use it up; wear it out; make it do; or do without.* I still wore a burgundy twill coat that Mother had made for me when I was five years old. Three years later it had been let out, pieced, and lengthened. The coat now pulled across my shoulders, and even the lengthened arms stopped three inches above my wrists. Oh, well. Coat weather did not last too long in southern Arizona.

We weren't poor. We just didn't have much money.

The Ranch was supposed to be a paying enterprise to supplement other income. Daddy had a paying job as an engineer inspector for the highway department. In reality, The Ranch extracted blood, sweat, and tears from his soul as well as cash from his pockets.

Folks who lived in farm labor camps were poor. Big farmers around us had three levels of poverty-stricken employees. First was a core staff, skilled farmhands and their families who labored through the seasons taking care of mundane yearlong tasks that a farm required – plowing, planting, weeding, harvesting, herding, milking. They lived in permanent enclaves. Their homes contained basic amenities for living. There was generally a community bath house for the residents. The more fortunate had personal bathrooms. These people were poor, but they had steady jobs and consistent roofs over their heads. Their children were enrolled in school all year.

The next group of employees that big farmers engaged were Mexican men who came from south of the border. *Braceros* worked in this country temporarily and legally to alleviate a war-time labor shortage. The program was being extended into post-war times. The men lived frugally in bunk houses or shared communal shacks. They sent most of their hard-earned dollars back to families in Mexico.

The rest of the farm workers were migrants who followed the crops – cotton, sugar beet, melon. Some trolled back and forth across the country between Oklahoma and California. Okies we called them. Others rattled in from Mexico in dilapidated Fords tied together with baling wire. Back seats squirmed with little brown children that seasonally flooded Washington School. These children were sent to Mrs. Peabody's class, an unofficial predecessor of the ESL program, because she spoke Spanish.

Migrant refugees set up camps near the fields. Some rolled in with rusty trailers. Others pitched tents. These camps often did not have even the crudest of amenities such as electricity, running water, or toilets.

At cotton picking time a field hand was paid 75 cents for picking 100 pounds of cotton. Picking cotton was, without a doubt, the most inhumane labor a person could perform. It was the last vestige of slave labor in this country. In stooped position, the harvester hand-picked fiber from stickery bolls and deposited it in a canvas sack that hung over his shoulder and dragged behind him. When the sack became heavy and hard to manage, he took it to the scales where a tally was kept. A good picker could pick 500 pounds a day, but he was the exception. The average picker did not do that well. It took an entire family picking cotton to keep body and soul together. Despite what Mother said, I could see that poor was not a state of mind. It was real.

One morning Mother and Daddy stood at the mail boxes. The mail was late this day. The field to the south looked like a sea of popcorn. Men, women, even children, had been working up and down the rows in McElroy's field since sunup. It was the height of cotton picking season, and laborers were pressed to garner the prime crop of Pima cotton lest it be destroyed by inclement weather. White canvas sacks bulged at their sides. Methodically their fingers snatched and bagged the feathery wisps from the capsules. The workers wore wide-brimmed hats for protection from the sun and long sleeved shirts for defense against burrs, barbs, and twigs of the cotton plants. In addition to watching what they were picking and doing it resourcefully, they had to watch their feet, for rattlesnakes were known to frequent the irrigated rows.

Mother shaded her eyes. A cloud of dust roiled down the road. But, it was not the mailman. It was a farm wagon pulling a trailer. On benches down the sides of the trailer hunkered a pack of stoic field workers. Empty canvas sacks draped over their shoulders. They were going to a cotton field.

Seeing Mother and Daddy standing at the mail boxes the driver of the wagon pulled to the side of the road.

"Are you folks lookin' fer a place to pick?" he yelled.

Mother gasped.

We were not *that* poor!

Are You Folks Lookin' For a Place To Pick?

Chapter 10
DENIZENS OF THE DESERT

The hottest place in the nation, the driest river, the least rainfall, the largest cactus, the smallest hummingbird, the most poisonous lizard. The Arizona desert proclaimed life in the superlative.

Our chickens were sequestered in cozy coops and behind mesh fences. Our human neighbors were few and far between. But, the land around us teemed with creatures that made the desert their sanctuary. They adapted quite simply to the harsh land. They found little hideouts where the sun couldn't get to them. Many were nocturnal and came out at night to forage or hunt. We often met them in the early hours of the day before they returned to their lairs. We were the interlopers who persisted in plodding through day after insufferable day.

After Mother tucked us into bed at night we heard Coyote "howlin' to the moon above." It was actually more usual to hear Coyote than to see him. This elusive member of the dog family transmitted secret messages through eerie quavering back-and-forth yodels. Sometimes mournful sobs were punctuated by sharp yelps or harsh barks. If we were to get a glimpse of Coyote we would see a light grey animal about the size of a small Collie slinking over the terrain with his proverbial tail tucked between his legs. The position of his tail immediately distinguished Coyote from Dog who ran with his tail up. Coyote was a night-time prowler. An omnivore, he was an opportunistic hunter making meals of small mammals, lizards, and birds as well as grapes and melons from nearby fields. Occasionally, in a pack, Coyote cooperated in hunting something larger like a deer or a calf. We could attest to the fact that he also ate barnyard fowl! Periodically, on an early morning survey of our kingdom, we would see a trail of feathers suggesting a macabre demise of one of our feathered friends.

If we watched quietly, we might see Jackrabbit bounding between brittlebush and bursage. He was an audacious character so like Br'er Rabbit of legend. His hind legs, longer than his fore legs, allowed him to leap and zigzag at great speeds to avoid natural predators. Mark Twain brought Jackrabbit's name to fame in his book of western adventure, *Roughing It*. Jackrabbit's exceedingly long ears, equated to jackass ears, served as antennae and helped him cool himself via a fine network of veins and capillaries.

His cousin, Cottontail, was more timid. Cottontail was stockier and softer appearing than his hare counterpart. He hopped slowly. His ears were short. And, his signature white cotton-ball of a tail was his identifying trait. Cottontail, like Jackrabbit, took his diet from coarse bark, twigs, and buds of the desert. But he also raided lettuce fields and became problematic for our neighboring farmers.

Ground squirrels darted from their burrows. They had a tendency to rise on their hind legs to survey the terrain. In moments of distress they warned family members of impending danger by emitting sharp screeching cries.

Of the assorted other rodents that frequented The Ranch, the most detrimental was Gopher. He lived most of his life underground. We never saw the creature, but we identified him by his work. A large horseshoe-shaped mound signaled the entrance to his intricate burrow system beneath the surface of the land. These gopher tunnels could damage water lines and irrigation pipes as well as tree roots. Gopher tunnels also harbored rattlesnakes. The vipers of the wasteland did not create their own lairs. They occupied ready-made holes and burrows built by other denizens of the desert. When a new gopher mound appeared in the main ranch yard Daddy set a trap, a contraption like a Chinese twister puzzle. It had lethal claws that squeezed the gopher when tripped. A nasty end to a disagreeable pest.

Various lizards sunned themselves on rocks and fence rails. They occasionally flicked their tongues at ants and insects that happened into their proximity. The collared lizard and the desert iguana resembled miniature dinosaurs and would have been terrifying were their sizes increased to such gigantic proportions. As it was, they were but skittish reptiles that, with a flip of their tails, disappeared instantly into cracks between rocks when they were startled.

The one reptile that Cricket and I regularly caught was Horny Toad. His name was a misnomer because he was not a toad. His round body and blunt snout made him resemble a flat toad. He had spines on his back and sides and protruding horns above his eyes. His appearance was most formidable, but he was generally a lethargic lizard. He sat in wait for slow moving insects, spiders, and sow bugs, then with a lash of his long sticky tongue captured his prey. Because of Horny Toad's docile character Cricket and I could capture him between our palms and transfer him to the temporary confines of a shoe box.

We developed a live and let-live attitude toward most of the desert dwellers. Only those that were actually dangerous or deleterious to our well-being did we actively deter. The rattlesnake was one in point. Periodically we encountered a rattlesnake on The Ranch. And where there was one, legend had it, there was another nearby.

We all had our near-encounters with snakes. Early spring was the season they began stirring after a winter's hibernation. The first spring after we moved to The Ranch, Mother and Cricket were transferring a hose to water the citrus trees. Mother asked Cricket to scoot under the low canopy of a grapefruit tree to knock off a small sucker shoot that was branching from the base of the tree. Whereupon, Cricket came nose to nose with a Western Diamondback Rattler coiled like a rope. How Mother retrieved Cricket unscathed is an unexplained miracle. Mother grabbed a shovel and beheaded the viper with a single blow. His was the first in a line of snake skins that dangled from barbs on the back fence.

The rattlesnake's diet was primarily small rodents; however lizards and small birds were sometimes impaled by the rattler's stunning venom before he gulped them down whole. We learned from experience that a rattlesnake would eat a small chicken as well as consume hen eggs.

One morning I went with Mother to the barn where we stored extra bags of chicken feed. As we opened the corral gate leading to the barn a whip-like object hurled through the opening. Before our stunned eyes, a loop of the whip thrust forward as the end of the whip pushed into the earth. It was a snake propelling sideways. It whipped over the sand like an egg beater and left a distinctive trail of parallel j-shaped lines.

"Oh, Good God!" Mother gasped. And it didn't sound prayerful.

A Sidewinder, we were to learn, was a rattlesnake that had adapted to the sandy soils of the desert. That he was on our ranch was a bit unusual because of the hard-pan nature of our land. This was a snake that got away. For a long time we were skittish about going into the barn.

We were conditioned to exercise caution when playing or working about The Ranch. Reclusive rattlers tended to avoid contact with humans if possible. They struck only when threatened. Generally, our policy was to retain a respectful separation from the serpent. However, confrontational Tige, whose name, by now, had been abbreviated to the first syllable of Tiger, had a lesson to learn. One afternoon Tige scuttled to the house yelping. He pawed pathetically at his throat. He had come face to face with a rattlesnake and refused to back down until the rattler had grazed his throat with her fangs.

In the ensuing hours Tige's throat swelled like a bullfrog's. He sought refuge under the tamarisk trees and whimpered and whined. He left his food untouched. As days passed Tige limped from his sanctuary and mooned about the ranch. Was he going to live? Time proved that Tige would survive the snakebite. He emerged from the experience a chastened hound who avoided rattlesnakes like the rest of us.

Other creepy crawlies that created consternation in our lives were venomous arachnids. Many a morning Mother found a small scorpion hugging the wall of the bathroom shower. The Arizona Bark Scorpion was usually found under rocks, logs, tree bark, and other surface objects and litter. He was also the scorpion most commonly encountered in houses. Of the numerous varieties of scorpions found in Arizona, the bark scorpion had the most medically serious sting.

"Shake out your shoes before you put them on," Mother admonished every morning.

We also shook our blue jeans and shirts, particularly if we had dropped them on the floor before we went to bed. Mother, Daddy, and I were all pegged by scorpions while we lived on the ranch. My encounter resulted in a flight to the doctor. Later encounters were taken in stride. Mother was stung at night as she slept. A little scorpion dropped from the wall onto the bed. Mother's face was resting on her hand. The toxic devil impaled her at the base of her thumb and again on her neck. Daddy was stung while he sifted through debris around The Ranch. A stabbing pain, slight local swelling, and faint red spots, which were puncture points, were the initial symptoms. Nausea, perspiration, tremors, and fever turned out to be minimal if the site was immediately covered with an ice pack.

We were also watchful for Black Widows. They were reclusive spiders that constructed thick, irregular webs of strong sticky silk. Black Widow webs were typically situated under ledges, near the ground, in dark and sheltered sites. The jet-black female hung belly upward in the center of her web. She had a globular abdomen that was marked by a bright red hour-glass shaped spot. Her wicked reputation purported that she consumed her consort spider after mating. We found numerous Black Widow lairs in the barn, in wood piles, even under furniture that had not been moved in a while. We never had the misfortune of being bitten.

One afternoon I was playing in the shade of the laundry shed. Clinging to the wall of the shed was a hairy creature that looked like a fiend from a horror movie. It was as big as a dinner plate; eight hirsute legs splayed from his abdomen.

Spiders, in general, triggered a primordial segment of my brain that radiated danger. Seeing one large enough to consume a turkey poult made my hair stand on end. Here was a lonely Tarantula. Daddy captured Mr. Hairy Legs in a coffee can and transferred him further into the desert where he could take up residence in a gopher hole.

Maybe Tarantula was pretty harmless to humans. His bite, supposedly, had an effect much like a wasp sting, swelling and mild pain for a few hours. Harmless phooey! Even if his bite wouldn't kill me, surely the shock of being tasted by such a giant spider would!

Chapter 11

WHO RULES THE ROOST?

"You'll have to ask your mother."
"Ah, Daddy. It's supposed to be funny."
I thought Daddy would be a push-over if I ask him if I could go to *The Boogie Man Will Get You* with my friend Sharon. I'd need fifteen cents if I went.
"Check with your mother then."
Daddy was adequate. He was tolerant but aloof. There wasn't much he could do except work and read and figure. When he wasn't out among the chickens, hauling feed, cleaning buildings, checking water lines, repairing fences, he was pouring over poultry journals or rolls of highway plans. He paced the kitchen with a pencil behind his ear and scratched rows of numbers on columnar pads.

Often Daddy was away. His job sites took him to the four corners of Arizona, and we only saw him when he wound his way home late on Friday nights. Occasionally, construction sites were within traveling distance from our ranch, and for a period of time, Daddy would bounce in at sunset, help Mother check the chicken houses, deal with ranch business, fall into bed, rise at the crack of dawn, and be on the road again. There were times Daddy was confined to the Highway Department offices in Phoenix to prepare reports. Then we saw him a bit more regularly.

Daddy's saving grace was that he could stand on his

head. In jovial times he entertained us with this acrobatic feat. Cricket mastered the skill, and sometimes we'd witness Big Bill and Little Bill upside down on the kitchen floor. I tried to assume a headstand. Either my position was wrong or my center of gravity was misplaced for I consistently splattered on my backside in the mode of a square somersault.

Once Daddy boasted that he could execute a swan dive. I called him to task at McElroy's pond. Daddy wavered at the edge of the pool as I ragged him to perform the graceful plunge. To placate his annoying child, Daddy belly-flopped into three feet of water below. I was decidedly underwhelmed at his awkward plummet.

Mostly Daddy was gone. He brought us books of a classic nature, *Treasure Island;* or of a historic nature, *The Lewis and Clark Expedition;* or of a regional nature, *The Waterless Mountain.* He asked about school; he checked arithmetic papers; and he reached into his pocket to give us a dime each week. He left child-rearing and discipline to Mother.

Mother was determined that Cricket and I be prepared to function in polite society. She set the table for evening meals. We wiped our mouths with cloth napkins.

We bowed our heads for grace. *"We Thank, Thee, O Lord, for these and other blessings..."* When Daddy was there he tacked on *"Amen! Brother Ben! Shot at a goose and killed a hen!"* and Cricket and I snickered.

Mother pushed manners: "Use a fork. Were you were born in a barn?"

... and family: "Of course you love him. You are his sister."

... and friends: "You can't pick your family, but you can pick your friends."

... and chores: "The kitchen will not sweep itself."

... and nourishment: "Eat your peas; there are children starving in China."

Mother made sure that we were clean: "Just look at the dirt on the back of your neck!"

... and dressed for the occasion: "I'm cold. Put your sweater on."

... that we did our schoolwork: "Correct your mistake; that's why your pencil has an eraser."

... that we were culturally astute: "Practice that scale again. Middle C is in the same place that it was yesterday."

... that we were good natured: "Stop crying or I'll give you something to cry about."

... that we were prudent: "What were you thinking when you did that?"

... that we were behaved: "Go out and get me a switch!"

Mother's logic was indisputable and final: "Because I said so. That's why!"

Mother took us on the last streetcar ride in downtown Phoenix. She taught us how to view a solar eclipse. She baked cupcakes for school parties, led a Brownie Troop, and kept score for the Little League Team.

In general, we were accountable to Mother.

Chapter 12
CHICKEN SOUP

"Yeow!" I screeched as Mother daubed my knee with turpentine. Mother figured if turpentine would remove color from your paint-smeared hands it would remove a few germs from a skinned knee. It would have to do in lieu of rubbing alcohol.

For the most part Mother took care of our bumps and bruises, our sniffles and coughs, our aches and pains. The logistics of a fifteen-mile drive into Glendale discouraged frivolous jaunts for medical advice. The exceptions were periodic appointments for Cricket who suffered from respiratory problems and from an agonizing rash that the doctors called eczema. Mother took him to Dr. Johnson at designated intervals. Cricket's remedies included a cache of balms and elixirs that required refills from the pharmacy. Luckily, the rest of us were hale and hearty. We relied on Mother's medicine arsenal to keep it that way.

Mother's medicine box included Band-Aids, gauze rolls, adhesive tape, aspirin, and witch hazel. On occasion, if I complained of a belly ache, Mother pulled out mineral oil because I needed "flushing." If I had a sore throat she mixed a concoction of vinegar (or lemon juice in season), honey, and cayenne. If I had a toothache she dipped a cotton ball in clove oil, and I clinched it on the affected spot. If anything had to be disinfected she doused it with Lysol.

Mother operated on splinters and cactus spines with needle, tweezers, and a paring knife. "God Bless Me," I wailed as I dangled over a kitchen stool while Mother worked on a cluster of cholla thorns embedded in my backside.

For the most part I kept my aches and pains to myself because the cure was usually worse than the affliction.

Earache: two drops of onion juice in the affected auricle. Sunburn: Rub with straight vinegar. Ant bites: Wipe with ammonia. Cough: Mixture of molasses, peppermint oil and two teaspoons of whiskey. Headache: a damp washcloth over the eyes and take a nap.

The best part of Mother's remedies was the pot of chicken soup she inevitably put on the back burner of Butane Stove when one of us got sick. It started with a whole chicken, so the rich broth was laced with thick chunks of meat. The recipe was never the same. It depended upon the vegetables that we had on hand what went into the soup – onions, celery, carrots, beans, turnips, tomatoes. Before the soup finished simmering, Mother tossed in a handful of rice. Chicken soup was the sure-cure for ailments ranging from headache to ingrown toenails.

Daddy never got sick. But one morning he staggered out to the breakfast table.

"I'b sick," he groaned. "Ghhrrrgh, ghhrrrgh," a fearful cough originated in his chest.

Mother hhmphed. This meant that she would have to transfer the cockerels to a holding pen by herself. "Go on back to bed," she said tersely.

Daddy returned to the bedroom and pulled a blanket under his chin. Through the walls we could hear anguished groans punctuated by raucous snorts. "Ghhrrrgh, ghhrrrgh."

Mother went about her tasks. The cockerels were in a restless mood; one particularly fractious cock ended up in Mother's soup kettle where he bubbled and stewed for the remainder of the morning.

Mother returned to Daddy intermittently. Daddy shivered with ague. She gave him an aspirin. Daddy's throat was like sandpaper. She mixed a gargle of vinegar, honey, and cayenne.

Daddy's cough raged on. "Ghhrrrgh, ghhrrrgh."

At lunch time Mother served Daddy a cup of her chicken soup.

"I beliebe I'b gedding bedder," Daddy whispered when Mother again entered the bedroom with one of her potions. She dosed him with a tincture of molasses, peppermint oil, and Jack Daniels. Late in the afternoon, Daddy emerged from the house. He was dressed and ready to help with the cockerels. Admittedly, he still looked green around the gills, and he wheezed like a rasp against a blackboard. "Ghhrrrgh, ghhrrrgh."

Daddy, too, had decided Mother's cures were worse than his affliction. Personally, I believed it was the chicken soup that put Daddy on the road to recovery, or maybe it was an extra dose of Jack Daniels.

Some calamities defied Mother's voodoo approach to the healing arts. One summer afternoon I was engrossed in a tale from India. In the story, a fakir lay meditating on a bed of nails. I idly asked Mother why the nails didn't hurt him.

Mother explained, "If the nails are close enough together no single nail will pierce the man." Then she added, "But, it doesn't sound like a very comfortable bed."

This mysterious concept puzzled me. I decided to try my own bed of nails. I sought the supplies in the garage. On a dusty shelf, amid the riffraff, I located a can containing widgets and gidgets, screws and brads. It held an odd assortment of nails, long and short, thick and thin, steel, brass, and galvanized. Some were decidedly bent as if they had been pulled from prior projects. Some were rusted. The garage did not harbor a piece of wood as big as a bed, but I did find a slat from a citrus crate and decided that a miniature bed of nails would suffice. I had the necessary items for my project.

I tacked five or six spikes across one end of the board. Some of the nails bowed before they were knocked through. I could see that covering even a small board with nails would take a long time. I began pounding pegs indiscriminately over the surface of the wood. Ragged, rusty spikes protruded in slapdash directions.

I soon tired of the carpentry part of my experiment. I was ready to test my bed of nails. I untied my oxfords. Brown oxfords, splitting from the sole. I peeled off my socks. Blue socks fraying at the toes. I resolutely planted my right foot in the center of the board. Two nails perforated my heel. One sliced the side of my foot. I rocked forward, and the arch of my foot rode over a wicked barb. I howled in anguish. The spike impaling my arch had not released, and the board dangled from my foot. When I pulled the offending nail (and board) from my foot, a geyser of blood spewed over the garage floor.

I hobbled to the house in tear-stained agony. Mother's fury at what I had done was tempered only by her fear of the effects of tetanus. She hustled me into the car and carted me to Dr. Johnson.

"My younger brother got lockjaw after he stepped on a nail," Mother wailed. "You have to have a tetanus shot."

I realized later that Mother's brother had not survived his bout with tetanus.

When we returned home from our impromptu jaunt to Glendale, Mother dispatched a raucous cockerel and plopped him in a bubbling kettle on the back burner of Butane Stove.

On another occasion, I carried a stack of books to the hedge of tamarisk trees beside the barn. Their dusty branches hung to the ground and shielded Cricket and me when we played. I spread a blanket under the trees and sat down to read.

Almost immediately, as I shifted my weight on the blanket, I experienced a scorching pain on my left calf. I had offended a small scorpion. He had a long body with pincers in front and a thin segmented tail tipped with a venomous stinger. He left his tell-tale stinger in my calf. I began to exhibit the classic symptoms of the sting – swelling, numbness, tingling. Mother, again, carted me to Dr. Johnson. Little bumps popped up around the sting site. My eyes twitched and began to swell shut. Dr. Johnson bathed my wound, checked my tetanus schedule, and advised me to keep ice packs on the distressed spot. He presented Mother with a vial of a revolutionary drug that was just entering the medical market. Antihistamines were being newly prescribed to combat allergic reactions to irritants such as pollen, dander, and insect bites. Mother parsimoniously doled out the wonder pills that would relieve the swelling of my throat and eyes, and then she plied me with chicken soup.

    On a subsequent occasion Daddy was nailed by Scorpio's brother. No need to go to the doctor. This time Mother went straight to the ice pack and the precious antihistamines to treat Daddy's affliction. Again, a pot of chicken soup laced with onions, carrots, and beans bubbled and plopped to commemorate the ailment.

    One summer morning Daddy was on the road (again). Neighbor Eastman had stopped by the house. He walked with Mother across the road to Cantankerous Well. If neighbors had a common bond, it dealt with wells, water levels, and corroded pumps. Cricket and I tagged along after them. Mother reached for the pump switch that set forth a chain of events drawing water to the land.

    Unbeknownst to Mother a rubber belt that connected the main gears of the pump had slipped. Little Cricket saw the egregious fault and set about to fix the error. He grabbed the belt just as Mother flipped the switch. The large gear began spinning. The loose belt whipped erratically, then yanked Cricket under the grinding cog. Split seconds passed before Eastman slammed the switch off. The unchecked gear sliced Cricket's scalp on several rotations. By the time the gears came to a halt, Little Cricket's head was covered with blood.

    No telephone. No emergency rescue crews. No ambulance. Mother and Eastman trundled us the eternal miles to Glendale. They wheeled into a NO PARKING zone on the street in front of Dr. Johnson's office. They raced in carrying limp little Cricket.

    I, initially, was left in the car. My nose was pressed against the window as I awaited word of what was going on in the doctor's office. I bounced impatiently from one corner of the back seat to the other.

    Meanwhile, a Glendale Policeman was making his rounds of the city streets. He saw a green Oldsmobile flagrantly occupying a NO PARKING section of the curb. He stopped behind the offending Oldsmobile and got out of his patrol car. I cowered on the floor. Officious Officer pulled a ticket book out of his shirt pocket and proceeded to inscribe a notice of violation to the driver of the car.

Eventually, I was called into the doctor's office to wait out the ordeal. Several tense hours passed. When Cricket emerged from the doctor he was groggy from sedation. A series of stitches embroidered his crown. A gauze dressing swaddled his head. I was decidedly envious of Cricket's elevated status as preeminent invalid.

Mother was decidedly miffed at receiving a parking ticket.

She returned home, set a kettle on the stove, and headed to the coop to select an unfortunate bird for the ubiquitous chicken soup.

Chapter 13
AND NOT A DROP TO DRINK

"Someone is having water problems," Daddy mused.

We watched a water tanker chug past The Ranch, likely heading to Blanding's place one mile down the road.

The seven little spreads that radiated from the Black Canyon Stage Route depended on derelict wells to sustain life. When a pump broke down, when the water table was low, when innumerable disorders that affected the flow of water were not patched, the little rancher had to bring water to his spread via tanker truck. It was an expensive way to sustain a few chickens. Butch Brown provided such a service. Butch also pumped out septic tanks. He assured us that he used a different truck for each service.

Water problems generally occurred in the summer time. By 5:30 El Sol was up. He tossed his rosy bedcovers across the eastern sky then poked his head over the mountain ridge. Sunrise was but a fleeting episode on summer mornings. Desert air was crisp, dry, and deceptively invigorating.

The Ranch yard drifted to life. A rooster crowed. His harem began to rustle. The flock demanded breakfast. By mid-morning we knew the day would be a scorcher.

"The weatherman says it'll be 109° today." Daddy leaned against the hoe he was using in his long-standing battle against jimson weed. He wiped his brow and watched the desultory flocks peck about in their enclosures. El Sol was well on his rotation across the sky. Corrugated roofs of the ranch buildings reflected his defiant stare.

Tamarisks dropped skirts of needles around their ankles. Palo verdes withdrew yellow canopies of spring and now scattered leaves and twigs across the floor. Desert hearty cactus, the saguaro, the prickly pear, the cholla, hunkered in for what evolution had taught them, to stand dormant through long sieges of drought.

It was times like this when the valiant well could no longer elicit moisture from below the earth; when the pipes gasped; when rust spit from the channels.

A well began to deteriorate as soon as it was put into service. From the beginning it was a project with diminishing returns. It became encrusted, corroded, and eroded. Sometimes a well picked up mineral deposits from ground water and spouted muckish brown liquid. Certain conditions caused the water to be fizzy. Sometimes the water smelled like rotten eggs. A combination of disparate factors finally brought well-water to a trickle.

Then, there were pump problems. Sometimes the problem was as simple as replacing a blown fuse. Other problems were mechanical or electrical. More expensive repairs were needed.

It was only a matter of time before the stalwart contraption that brought water to our land chugged and gasped and refused to draw another drop. Butch Brown delivered a tank of water to The Ranch.

In the West, wars were waged over water. When our well succumbed to the vagaries of desert existence, Daddy donned his fighting gloves and began a war of his own. Daddy's method of battle was to study water tables, to pour over water laws, to research water associations, to contact well-drilling companies. He figured that the only way to prosper in the desert was to have a well like those of the big farmers.

And Not a Drop To Drink

John Jacobs and McElroy drilled deep into the bowels of the earth. They installed leviathan pumps that throbbed and pulsed, pushing water through 24" pipes, spewing it into canals that carried it to distant sections. Several of these pumps were positioned at critical corners of their land. Water was diverted to fields of alfalfa, cotton, soybeans, to lettuce, carrots, melons. It was directed to water troughs, feed lots, and dairies, to cattle and horses and sheep. It was piped to their labor camps and to their ranch headquarters. I suppose the big guys had water problems, too. Probably their wells malfunctioned and broke down on occasion, and we were insensitive to their plight. But they did have back-ups. We did not.

Daddy brought a pump service out to evaluate our situation. Daddy and the pump expert circled the well. They knocked on rusty brads and pistons. They stroked their chins. They hemmed and hawed. They scratched elaborate formulas into the sand. Band-Aid repairs might be made to this

Box 7, Black Canyon Stage Route

contrivance, but it would be prudent to put our money into a new well.

Daddy was far sighted. He envisioned a cooperative irrigation district with a well the magnitude of McElroy's or John Jacobs'. He sat at the kitchen table late into the night. He studied the covenants of successful irrigation cooperatives. He scribbled on his columnar pad. He came up with a plan, prices, payments, regulations. He would make a proposal to our six far-flung neighbors, dogged little guys like us, scraping by on subsistence homesteads, that we form The Black Canyon Stage Route Irrigation District. We could cooperatively dig a well that would rival the wells of our mega-farmer neighbors. Daddy would donate our acreage across the road to the Irrigation District for the site of the well.

Daddy approached Blanding.

"Sorry, Bill. I've just put my money into repairing the well that I have."

Daddy went to see Whitfield.

"Sorry, Bill. My pockets are not that deep."

Eastman.

"Sorry, Bill. My well is still drawing."

"Sorry."

"Sorry."

"Sorry."

Dejected, discouraged. Daddy lamented the provinciality of our neighbors. They didn't see the big picture. A more efficient water system would benefit all of us. Some even suggested that Daddy was appealing to the neighbors for aid with his own water problems.

Daddy would have to dig a well, but it would not be the automaton he had envisioned. The new well would be drilled on the side of the road where the ranchstead proper was located. The vacant parcel across the road, where the original well was located, would eventually be sold to finance Daddy's new well.

Daddy called Deep Enough Drillers. They came out with Dirk the Diviner. Dirk brought a pair of slim L-shaped rods that looked like bent coat hangers. With his wands of wizardry,

Dirk paced the property. He held one rod in each hand, the short part of the L held upright, and the long part pointing forward. Occasionally the rods twitched or wavered.

Cricket and I trailed after Dirk and shouted words of encouragement as the rods danced about making divine projections.

"There it goes," Cricket whooped.

Daddy stood in the middle of the yard with his hands on his hips. Dirk's divining rods eventually pointed to a spot near the east fence.

"This har's most likely the spot what you should dig," Dirk announced.

The divined spot was actually in the vicinity of where Daddy had hoped to locate the well!

Never-the-less, before Daddy would commence to dig, he called a geologist to discuss the site of the new well. George the Geologist brought topographical maps, augers, and probe rods. He assessed the terrain of The Ranch. He speculated about underground rock strata.

George the Geologist's scientific assessment brought him to the same spot along the east fence as had Dirk's divining rods. At this spot it would also be easy to pipe into our existing water lines.

Scientific enlightenment or divine intervention? In this case they pointed the same direction.

Deep Enough Drillers rattled in; a flat-bed truck carried mechanisms for boring into the earth. Masts, winches, rods, cables, sheaves, drill stems, bits.

And, Daddy sent us to the mountains. Mother, Cricket, and I would have a vacation. We luxuriated in a rustic cabin along Oak Creek. We reveled in cool, wooded seclusion. We splashed in sparkling waters. It was too bad that Daddy could not be with us.

Meanwhile, back at The Ranch, Daddy dealt with daily water-delivery by Butch Brown, with quenching the thirsty throats of the menagerie, and with well-drilling.

One evening the manager of Oak Creek Cabins rattled the door of the unit where Mother, Cricket, and I were staying.

"Miz Harrison. Yore husband called you. He wants you to call him back at this number as soon as possible."

We hastened to the office. Mother rang the operator and placed a long-distance phone call to the number the manager had given her. It could only be grave circumstances that would trigger a phone call from Daddy at this hour. Daddy was waiting at a payphone booth in Glendale where he had initiated the call.

"Whew," Daddy gasped. "I was afraid you would not get my message."

Mother braced for the worst.

"During the drill today a cable broke," Daddy said.

"Oh, Deah!" was Mother's response.

"The drill stem and bit did not come up."

"Oh, Deah!"

"They lodged at the bottom of the shaft, probably 10 or 12 feet down."

"Oh, Deah!"

"Deep Enough Drillers left in a snit abandoning the damned boring parts."

"Oh, Deah!"

"If the drill stem and bit were not retrieved we'd have to start a new dig."

"Oh, Deah!"

"It would double the cost of drilling the well."

"Oh, Deah."

"But, I got it out!" Daddy exclaimed. "After the drillers left I worked over the hole. I used every hook and probing device we had on The Ranch. I caught the frayed cable and inch by inch jimmied the drill stem and bit out of the hole. The drillers will be back tomorrow!"

Grit, tenacity, and ingenuity had saved the day. Daddy's elation over his conquest had prompted him to bounce into Glendale late at night and share his success long-distance.

When Mother, Cricket, and I returned to The Ranch after a week of repose, a new water system greeted us. A tidy cast iron pump with pressure switches, valves, tubes, plugs, impellers and diffusers hummed merrily away. And, cool, clear water ran from the kitchen faucet.

Chapter 14
THE PAHLAH

Digging a new well was an unforeseen expense. Daddy wanted The Ranch to be a self-sustaining operation. He decided to sell the property across the road to cover the expense of digging a new well. However, that small acreage bristling with prickly pear and cholla had absolutely nothing to recommend it without a house. Daddy decided to move Big House across the road. Newly stuccoed Big House.

Naturally, moving a house took planning and groundwork. Ever the engineer, Daddy spent a week scratching out drawings and entering figures on his familiar columnar pad. A foundation had to be prepared on the new site. Daddy dug massive holes that would be filled with cement. Upon these pilings Big House would rest. Mother worked right along side hauling dirt.

Daddy ordered a load of Redi-Mix concrete. A giant truck with a massive revolving drum pulled up and expelled heavy concrete into the holes. Mother wielded a trowel to smooth the rough substance.

Pipes had to be connected from the new Big House site to the well on that property. A septic tank had to be dug. Mother held pipes while Daddy joined the fittings.

In fact, the old pump had to be resurrected so that Big House would have water. More tinkering and cajoling a well that Daddy had abandoned in favor of a new one. Mother rolled up her sleeves and got her hands greasy with tasks more suited to a mechanic.

Time neared for Big House move. First, we had to move. We moved to Little House. But, not before Mother extracted a promise that Daddy would make an addition to our new residence.

Room by room we transferred our belongings from Big House to Little House. From kitchen to kitchen went the drop-leaf table and four chairs, ice-box, and Butane Stove. From living room to living room went upright piano, walnut rocker, and army-cot davenport. From bedroom to bedroom went maple bedstead, cedar chest, and bureau drawers. From Big House to Little House dishes, groceries, clothes, bedding, books, pictures, rugs, brooms, mops, and toothbrushes were transferred to their respective new locations.

Another big truck pulled into the yard. It was equipped with massive jacks and steel beams. Several stalwart men accompanied the truck. As far as house-moving was concerned Big House must have been an easy project. By the end of the day the house was lifted from its original foundation and set upon jumbo wheels and steel girders. The next day it was trolleyed across the road and solemnly set upon the new foundation. Daddy was particularly proud that his new stuccoing job did not crack in the transfer.

Even after the successful transfer, Big House was not ready for habitation. Plumbing lines had to be connected. Electrical lines had to be installed. An entire summer was consumed in relocating Big House.

The business of The Ranch continued as before. Another flock of pullets went to market. Another chicken house was scrubbed and sterilized. A new brood of chicks was installed.

Big House was listed "For Sale" in the classified ads of the *Republic*.

Eventually another hardscrabble family found our little plot with a fine stucco house and decided to throw their lot to the desert.

Thus, we had settled into funky Little House.

"We need a proper place to entertain," Mother moaned.

Did Mother expect white-gloved ladies to leave their calling cards on the hall table? Living room, sitting room, drawing room, lounge. The room where we gathered at the end of the day was one and the same, only Mother called it The Pahlah (the Parlor). It couldn't even be called the front room because the entrance to our four-room house was through the kitchen. Kitchen, Pahlah, Bathroom, Bedroom. If you walked through the house you found yourself exiting a bedroom door that was right next to the kitchen door. Perhaps early pioneers on The Ranch intended family living to occur in the kitchen and family sleeping to occur in the remaining rooms. However, Mother insisted upon a Pahlah.

The Pahlah contained an unharmonious arrangement of things makeshift and refined. The small room was dwarfed by a Howard upright piano circa 1900. That very piano had followed Daddy's parents from Arkansas to Colorado to Arizona as they ventured West prior to Arizona's statehood. I hadn't known my grandparents. They died during my wee years. World War II followed, and Daddy put into storage disparate fragments of their household. The piano along with other odd furnishings was retrieved and carted to The Ranch.

In the evenings Mother sat upon a small walnut rocker where she became absorbed in radio shows. Daddy had bought a deluxe Philco for us before he went to war. Its state-of-the art vacuum tubes relayed radio waves from around the world. Through the war years Mother kept it tuned to *News on the Home Front* and President Roosevelt's *Fireside Chats*. Now she listened to variety shows like *Lux Family Theater* and suspense dramas like *The Shadow*.

Cricket and I sat on the pahlah floor. We chuckled through the exploits of *Amos 'n Andy* or were captivated by the daring adventures of *The Lone Ranger*.

"We need another pahlah chair," Mother mused. Daddy, instead of sitting with us in The Pahlah, took his books to the kitchen where he hunched over the table and scratched calculations by dim overhead light.

Often Mother used her chair to rock and soothe Cricket.

His severe allergies rendered him uncomfortable and querulous. Mother spent endless hours comforting and stroking the agonizing itch that sometimes consumed Cricket's entire body.

A surplus army cot served as the davenport. By day it was covered by a boldly striped serape, a Mexican blanket of garish hues. By night, the cot was my bed. I pulled back the stiff coverlet and slipped between threadbare sheets. I was often aware of Mother rocking Cricket through the night. I listened to Mother croon and stroke while Cricket bellowed and squalled. Eventually Cricket nodded off, and Mother was able to take him into the bedroom and tuck him into another surplus cot positioned at the foot of the old maple bedstead.

The Pahlah was decorated in the mode of the West, only we didn't know that it was a style in those days. Navajo rugs carpeted the floor. They overlapped one another in a patchwork of discordant designs. My grandparents had accumulated a wild array of rugs that represented characteristic weaving patterns from different trading posts on the Navajo Reservation. The story was told that during my grandfather's young lawyering days in Flagstaff, he was occasionally paid for his legal services in rugs. Most of the rugs were frayed from years of foot traffic before Mother and Daddy spread them over our rough cement floor.

Other samples of handicrafts from Southwestern Indian tribes were jammed on window ledges and shelves along with framed daguerreotypes of unsmiling ancestors. Gourd rattles, stone ax heads, clay vessels, and coiled baskets vied for space among an oddment of objects like a silver compote, a satin pincushion, a Kodak Brownie, a slide rule, and a kerosene lamp.

Hopi bowls and Apache baskets were catch-alls for pencils and paper clips, shopping lists and receipts, loose screws, clothespins, marbles, and crayon stubs. They also contained caches of prehistoric arrow heads, stone drills, and shards from ancient earthenware that we occasionally found on the desert floor.

Mother hung white muslin curtains across the windows.

They did not cover the panes in any manner of privacy. Who needed privacy so far from civilization? They were simply white ruffles across the dusty sills.

The shelving of convention at The Ranch was citrus crates, the original modular furniture. Crates could be used upright or sideways. They could be nailed to the wall or stacked under a window. Crates were sturdy wooden divided boxes that created convenient shelves for books, towels, dishes, games, underwear, or cleaning supplies. They were useful as lamp tables, kiddies' desks, footstools, and general catchalls for the claptrap of our lives.

Books from Daddy's childhood lined the rough hewn shelves. A complete set of Oz books included not only *The Wonderful Wizard* but other volumes featuring characters like the *Tin Woodman* and *Ozma*. There were no girlie books. I grew up listening to tales like *Robin Hood* and *The Black Arrow*.

Sundry pieces of board games were lost and buried under the Navajo rugs or caught up in the miscellany of the catch-all baskets. Monopoly money and Parcheesi pawns, Domino tiles and Chinese Checkers marbles.

We practiced the piano in The Pahlah. Ear wrenching discords wafted over the desert as we protested practice time and made ditties like "Loudly Brays the Donkey" and "Row, Row, Row Your Boat" sound as horrible as possible.

Mother wanted a "reading chair" in The Pahlah – one that was soft, plush, and overstuffed – one in which she could curl up to read *The Saturday Evening Post* or novels from the Glendale Library. The possible answer to this furniture dilemma rested in the barn. An old Morris chair had been abandoned by former residents. It served as a roost for chickens, a nesting spot for mice, and a sleeping pad for a transient feline. Mother pulled the chair out into the yard, beat its frayed cushions and dusted its scarred arms. It was reasonably secure.

Mother envisioned the Morris chair as the focal point of The Pahlah. She would place it under the brass floor lamp whose top hat was a faded moiré shade. From the depths of her stitchery supplies, Mother produced a length of ticking, tight black and white striped fabric that was intended to cosset pillowcases and mattresses. For an entire afternoon Mother clipped and stitched. She covered the seat pad and the back of the chair with crisp material, unconventional for a Morris chair, but pleasing to the eye.

The chair was carted into The Pahlah and assumed a place of honor. Mother was pleased with her handiwork.

During the night, while the household was quiet, a transformation occurred in the chair. When the family trailed into The Pahlah next morning the chair was alive with spiders, white creatures with black spots on their abdomens. The *Encyclopaedia Britannica* told us that these were newly hatched Black Widows. Some would mature into those toxic femme fatales, glossy-black with a bright red hour-glass marking the undersides of their abdomens. The males would also bear the tell-tale hourglass, but they would be tan in color and less poisonous in nature. Perhaps conditions were right in our cozy house, or perhaps it was simply time for the creatures to emerge from their protective sacs.

Mother immediately dragged the chair out of the house, dusted it with insecticide, and eventually returned it to the barn where roosters, and rats, and itinerant cats took up residence again.

Chapter 15

ARE WE HAVIN' FUN YET?

Once relocated, Mother was not going to release Daddy from his promise to add more rooms to Little House. At night they sat in the kitchen and sketched plans on the oilcloth-covered table. The most sensible plan was to extend out from the kitchen. They would pour a large pad of cement. By adding a new Pahlah, and a proper bedroom for Mother and Daddy, and even an up-to-date bathroom, they would double the size of Little House. The kitchen would remain the same. The old Pahlah would become my official bedroom, and the existing bedroom would become Cricket's.

Mother looked forward to her improved home. On bits of paper she sketched room arrangements. She made lists of furniture and accessories she would like to buy. She designed curtains that she would hang in the windows.

Daddy still juggled his weekday highway department job and weekend chicken ranching job. Another flock of pullets went to market. Another chicken house was scrubbed and sterilized. A new brood of chicks was installed.

One day Daddy grabbed his pad of graph paper, stuck a pencil behind his ear, and put a tape measure in his pocket. He paced off from the kitchen door the approximate distance he expected to construct the addition to the house. He scratched and calculated on the graph paper. He measured again, this time with the tape. He drove wooden stakes around the path he had paced. He strung twine from stake to stake and tied little yellow flags on the twine.

The next weekend Daddy dug a trench around the perimeter. With pick and shovel he penetrated the hard caliche. Another weekend he built a wooden box around the entire excavation. And on yet another weekend, a big truck churning cement rolled into the yard and discharged its load, the foundation and floor of our new addition. Daddy and Mother spent the day spreading, then leveling, then finishing the heavy composite substance. Cricket and I drew our initials in one corner of the big concrete pad.

Life among the chickens went on. A flock of pullets went to market. The chicken house was scrubbed and sterilized. A new brood of chicks was installed.

The walls of the new addition never went up.

A flock of pullets went to market. The chicken house was scrubbed and sterilized. A new brood of chicks was installed.

* * *

There's nothin' to do," I whined.

"I can find something for you to do," Mother threatened.

Either I suddenly found a way to occupy my idle moments, or I'd be gathering eggs, scrubbing the bathroom sink, sweeping the cement pad, or raking the area around the back door.

Mother didn't organize play dates. There were long, lonely stretches under the sun when Cricket and I had to entertain ourselves. We rambled about in spaces that reached from here to eternity, but they lacked the whimsy of a park playground.

After each brood of chicks had been pampered from hatchling to marketable pullet, Mother and Daddy sterilized the building. Each new flock would be housed in a clean building, free of parasites or intrinsic fowl disease. Occasionally they let a house stand fallow. When that happened I was allowed to set up a play house.

I pulled boxes and crates from the garage, set up sawhorses and stretched rough planks across them, and collected tin cans to serve as cookware. I made a doll bed in a citrus crate. I went so far as to design a line of furniture that I figured Daddy could whip up for me in his spare time. This would replace my temporary estate and upgrade the playhouse.

"If Daddy could build furniture like that, I would have him make some for me," Mother laughed.

Sometimes I tried to force my squirrelly kid brother to be my next door neighbor, but he was a pathetic playmate. All he had to do was come over to borrow sugar and sit down for a cup of coffee. I provided him with Matilda, my second-rate doll, to bring along to play with my perfect doll, Agnes, who slumbered in her crib.

Cricket arrived at the chicken house door. Wham! Bang! He pounded with an angry fist. He gripped poor Matilda by one foot. This was not going the way I planned.

"Come in Mrs. Brown," I cooed.

Cricket sneered. "I'm not Mrs. Brown."

'You are for this visit," I reasoned. "Will you have a cup of coffee?"

"I don't drink coffee," Cricket retorted.

"Just for today," I implored. "This is pretend."

Cricket sulked. "I don't like your game of pretend."

"You said you'd play with me!" I glowered, feet apart and hands on hips.

"I don't want to be Mrs. Brown!" Cricket yelled.

I grabbed him by the collar. "This is my game. You have to play my way!"

Cricket jerked away. "Here's yer stupid doll." He flung poor Matilda across the room.

So much for neighborly visits.

When Daddy needed the chicken house for a new flock, I was forced to set up housekeeping elsewhere. Sometimes it was another coop, washed and sanitized, standing vacant for later residents. Or it might be under the weeping boughs of a cluster of tamarisks where Cricket and I had a tree house.

Daddy had nailed a small platform across the branches of a dusty tree. It had no side rails, but the brush of the tree provided a bit of security preventing a six-foot plunge to the ground. We took games up there. We sometimes carried our lunches and had impromptu picnics. I retreated to the tree house with my library books.

One day I convinced Cricket that we should spend the night in the tree house. The idea percolated in his little pea head before he, also, agreed this would be a grand adventure. The next step was to broach Mother and Daddy with the idea. That turned out to be harder than I imagined.

"No." Mother's unexplained response.

"That's not a good idea," Daddy hedged.

"Why?" I demanded.

And, we went round and round.

After days of my persistent prodding, Mother and Daddy relented. "Let them try it," Daddy conceded.

After dinner on a summer night Mother and Daddy, toting blankets and pillows, accompanied us to the tree house. Cricket and I, pajama-clad, danced along beside them. First, Daddy. He climbed the wooden slats nailed up the trunk of the tree and spread a blanket across the floor of the pallet. Then, Mother. She handed Daddy the pillows and immediately retreated down the steps. Then, Cricket and I scampered up the makeshift ladder. Daddy covered us with a second blanket and said goodnight. Mother blew us kisses from ground below. They returned to the house.

Moon light. Stars bright. Summer night. Cricket and I marveled at our new-found freedom. Lizards hurried. Rabbits scurried. Field mice flurried. Cricket's skinny little body became rigid. A sharp yodel pieced the air; then a mournful response echoed from a distance. Cricket quivered. Overhead, the branches of the tamarisk parted, and a Great Horned Owl dove landward, grasping an ill-fated rodent in his talons.

Cricket whispered, "I'm going back to the house."

"You can't go back," I hissed.

"I don't want to sleep here."

Cricket threw back the covers and scrambled down the ladder.

"Chicken!" I screamed upon his swift retreat.

I snuggled into a roomier repose in the lofty aerie.

Minutes passed. Daddy was at the base of the tree. "You'll have to come in, Susan. You can't stay here all night."

I raged. I pouted. I didn't want to go to the house. This was Cricket's fault. Our entire sleep-out expedition had not lasted half an hour.

There were occasions when the tables were turned. Cricket wanted to play Cowboys and Outlaws and I was his only choice for either a *compadre* or a foe. He and I strapped cap guns over our hips and sidled behind barrels and corral gates shooting at each other. I insisted on being Calamity Jane. Cricket assumed the role of Wild Bill Hickok. In real life Wild Bill wouldn't have been shooting at his ally and the disputed heroine of the plains, but we were somewhat loose in our interpretation of Wild West history.

City kids had sidewalks and roller rinks. One Christmas Cricket and I received roller skates. The kind that clamped on. The kind that tightened with special keys that dangled from dirty cords around our necks. The skates adjusted to our shoe sizes so they would grow with our feet. With the addition of the big cement pad extending from the kitchen door, Cricket and I had a skating rink.

I received a bicycle the Christmas I was nine years old. I had had some rudimentary balancing instructions on a bike at a friend's house, but certainly had not mastered the skill of remaining upright while the machine was in motion. My new bike was a shiny green, balloon-tired Spitfire. I rolled it from the Christmas tree and out the kitchen door. I swung my leg over the seat and shifted my weight to the right pedal. The bicycle began rolling toward a line of tamarisks. I could neither steer it nor stop it. I barreled into the arms of the waiting shrubbery. My greenhorn ride netted a permanent dent in the bike's front fender. After I refined my balancing and steering, the bike propelled me back and forth to the mail box and up and down country roads.

We even had access to a swimming hole. At one of his mega wells, McElroy widened the ditch and even cemented the sides of a makeshift pond. He secured a metal ladder down one side of the hole. When the well was pumping, water careened into the pond. It whirled and eddied filling the pool 'til it was chest high. It then exited through one of two culverts on opposite sides of the pool and continued along a ditch to a waiting field. Cool, clear, fresh water. Unfiltered, unchlorinated water.

McElroy was a generous neighbor. Romero was McElroy's foreman. Most of the neighborliness was transmitted via Romero. Romero oversaw the cultivating, planting, harvesting, and irrigating of such diverse crops as alfalfa, soybeans, cotton, lettuce, and carrots. Romero invited us to take afternoon plunges in McElroy's pond. On hot summer afternoons we looked forward to a dip in the refreshing water.

From the depths of her closet, Mother pulled out a moth-eaten garment that she wore to Alabama lakes during her debutante days. Misshapen, faded black wool, this was not the bathing attire of current models. On distant beaches the bikini was making a scandalous debut.

Mother wriggled into her habiliment and studied the figure reflected in the dresser mirror. She was not pleased. It was as if a girdle had been cut from an inner tube. It gripped her legs, strangled her torso, and pushed her bosom up to her chin. Mother pulled in her tummy; she slapped her thighs. She had gained a few pounds from when she last wore her swimming suit. My swimming suit was no different from my play suits. Light cotton jumpers with straps that buttoned over the shoulders were adequate for my aquatic antics.

It was sumptuous to be covered completely with water. At home our allotted three-minute showers did not permit us the luxury of total immersion. Sometimes Mother took a cake of soap to the swimming hole, and we lathered our arms, our legs, and even our hair. We were careful to do so at the pipe where water exited the pond. We did not want to contaminate the swimming area with suds.

Most of the time on The Ranch, we played alone. Cricket turned to his little boy toys, spades and pails, dump trucks and wagons, forts and tin soldiers. I turned to paper dolls, books, and diaries.

Chapter 16
OLD BILL

"Vamoose!"
"Hey!"
Cricket stood behind the barbed wire threads of the pasture fence. He watched McElroy's cowboys rounding up loose cattle. They dug their heels into the sides of dusty horses and circled the milling herd. Some waved hats; others swung lariats or bandanas.

Cattle ranged in the desert scrub behind our land. Strategically placed water tanks and salt blocks, as well as cattle guards built at crossroads, kept the livestock in a somewhat designated location. After winter rains they got nourishment from spring grasses and filaree. When the desert moved into drought mode, cowboys drifted through the land nudging hungry bovine into feed lots to fatten them for auction.

McElroy's cowboys were a rugged lot of *braceros*. They pinch-hit as ranch hands, mended fences, dug ditches, and branded cattle. Astride steeds of undetermined origin they now rode in search of strays.

The *braceros* embraced the uniform of the range. High peaked sombreros with broad brims offered sensible protection from the sun. Bandanas tied about their necks served as breathing masks or as insulation against the sun's rays. Ropes hung from their saddles in case stubborn cows needed persuasion.

"Vamoose!"

"Hey!"

A string of blistering profanities in Spanish peppered the air along with dust and pollen.

One believer in the cowboy mystique was Little Cricket. He hung over the fence and watched these western knights subdue the roiling herd. Cricket wanted to be a cowboy. He tossed aside previous career aspirations, a soldier, a garbage truck driver, a locomotive engineer. At almost-six-years-old he yearned to be a cowboy. For that he needed a horse.

"I need a horse," he yenned.

We were a fowl outfit. Our feathered assemblage consisted of thousands of White Leghorns that were being groomed for market as well as a coop of Rhode Island Red Hens that laid a smattering of breakfast eggs. By this time, we also had added to the menagerie a dozen turkeys destined for holiday tables, a family of ducklings, and two aggressive bantam roosters.

Besides Betty and her progeny, Tige, several other four-footed critters were also making their home on our spread: a couple of Easter rabbits, Boots and Whiffle; a wayward cat that set up mouse patrol in the barn, and a pig who escaped from Blanding's sty. (We returned the pig). And, for a while we had a lamb, courtesy of a Basque sheepherder.

But we did not have a horse.

Little Cricket hankered for a horse.

Roundup ended and desultory cattle plodded to new ground. Laconic riders followed in stride. A final "Vamoose!" "Hey!" punctuated the scene.

"I need a horse," Cricket pined sulkily.

As if on cue, Romero rattled into the yard. Not only did Romero manage the many crops on McElroy Farms, he, also, directed the herds. On this day the herd was being moved to greener pastures. Romero did most of his cowboying from a dented Ford pickup.

Romero extricated himself from behind the wheel.

"Buenos dias, Meez Harrison." He clasped his hat politely in his hand.

"Hello, Romero. How are you today?" Mother replied.

"Good. Good," Romero nodded. "And, how is leetle Creekeet?"

Little Cricket grinned at this motorized cowman.

Mother laughed, "He has been watching you move the cattle. Surely you saw him."

"Si, si. That is why I came today."

"Oh."

"Meester McElroy has an old horse in the field. A geentle horse that can no longer be used for round-up. We call him Old Bill. Would leetle Creekeet like to have Old Bill?"

Mother was caught up short. Certainly she was thinking of the White Leghorns, the Rhode Island Reds, the turkeys, the ducks, the bantams, the dogs, the rabbits. Plus an itinerant cat, a transient pig, and a lamb. Oh, no! Not a horse!

She didn't have time to protest.

Little Cricket lit up like Christmas lights. "Yea! Yea! Hip, hip, hooray! A horse!"

A horse. A horse. Of course. A horse.

The decision was made.

Old Bill came into our lives. We became a homestead of Bills— Daddy Bill, Little Bill, and now Old Bill.

Next morning, as promised, Old Bill ambled up the road. Pedro sat astride, bareback, his dusty boots dangled on either side of the docile mount. Old Bill swayed lazily. Clop. Clop. Snort. Pedro waved and grinned at Cricket who was a welcoming committee of one, hanging on the gate. Not far behind, a cloud of dust signaled that Romero followed in his power-driven mount. Horse and pickup arrived at the same time.

The transfer of livestock occurred with a few instructions and a shake of hands. Romero provided us with a bridle and a bale of hay.

Old Bill was a knock-kneed bag of bones held together by two sides of untanned leather. He was shaggy, black; grey whiskers peppered his muzzle. When he grimaced yellow ivory showed he was long in the tooth. Old Bill was of indeterminate pedigree. He had once been a general ranch horse, but he had outlived his usefulness. McElroy was cutting him from the line. We had basic accommodations for a horse. The shed that we loosely called the barn was where we stored chicken feed. It was a three-sided shelter that contained a crib and a water trough. A side pen, bordered by a tier of heavy planks, served as the corral. An adjacent three acres, fenced with four strands of fierce barbed wire, was a pasture studded with tufts of dry desert foliage. Mother now had to add oats and hay to her weekly shopping spree at the feed and seed store.

Cricket robbed Mother's larder of horsy treats, apples, carrots, and heads of lettuce, to seduce his new friend. Old Bill took a grudging liking to his new little cowboy. Mother had to slip the bridle over Old Bill's nose at harnessing time, but Cricket was adroit in bouncing onto his back from the corral gate. In the transfer of livestock (Old Bill) and tack (horse gear) we did not receive a saddle. This was but a minor impediment to Cowboy Cricket. Cricket's almost-six-year-old legs stuck out perpendicular from Old Bill's bare back. Boy and horse plodded around the back field. They graduated to the mile stretch of road from our front gate to the mail boxes. Cricket could even nudge Old Bill into a respectable canter. Cricket flattened himself along Old Bill's neck, grabbed a hank of shaggy mane, and galloped Apache-style along country roads.

Although the steed had a diet of hay and oats from the feed store as well as the purloined treats that Cricket slipped him, Old Bill resorted to another brand of munchies. He started eating the corral fence and gradually compromised the top rail.

The corral was simply a suggestion to keep Old Bill contained. Not only did he eat the rails and scratch himself obscenely against the rough boards, he amused himself by thumping against the gate. Occasionally, he knocked the latch loose, and in true old-horse fashion he headed back to the barn, McElroy's barn, impervious to what awaited him there. Romero or Pedro patiently led him once again to our estate.

I was not as nimble as Cricket in maneuvering Old Bill. When I took a notion to go for a horseback ride Old Bill snorted with disgust. With decided bad humor he allowed me to mount. Old Bill clumped and swayed with me on his back. With each step he sighed dismally. I was not able to nudge him beyond clop, clop, snort. He paused occasionally to deposit a load of horse nuggets or a fountain of hot urine. When I dismounted onto the corral gate he graced me with a slobbery prod that knocked me to the ground.

The only occasion where I excelled in a relationship with Old Bill concerned the care of his eyes. Horseflies buzzed around the stable. These mammoth insects that inspired the song "Blue Tailed Fly" were a menace in the corral. They attacked Old Bill in his most vulnerable spots, primarily around his eyes. Nasty sores erupted. A balm came in the form of a medicated tar that had to be daubed on the sore spots with small flat sticks or tongue depressors. Cricket claimed to be too little to perform the task. Old Bill balked at Mother's touch. The lot fell to me.

I tied the old geezer to a fence post and proceeded with the medicinal task. The horse stood patiently as I spread goo over the angry sores. In spite of the tenderness I exhibited in these nurturing moments, Old Bill did not return the favor if I tried to ride him. My riding relationship with him continued to be clop, clop, snort.

Clop. Clop. Snort.

Chapter 17
COWBOY CRICKET

The cowboy of lore wore a white Stetson, a red bandana, and silver spurs. He twirled a hemp lariat and strapped a six-gun over his hip. And, he wore pointy-toed, high-heeled boots.

Now that Cricket had a horse he amassed the gear of a cowboy. Assorted hats, bandanas, and ropes were scattered around The Ranch. They were generally useful items in any outdoor operation. But, the boots. Ah, the boots. Little Cricket begged for boots. Mother looked at Little Cricket's almost-six-year-old feet and expressed dismay at shodding them with frivolous footwear. So, she turned a deaf ear to his pleas and hoped that this phase would pass as did the soldier phase and the garbage man phase. Meanwhile, Cricket knotted a bandana at his throat, tipped a straw hat on his head, mounted his mustang via the corral fence, and cantered about The Ranch with his feet dangling in shaggy Keds.

Old Bill was as oblivious to the footwear problem as was Tige, who capered at the heels of horse and rider. At an early age Tige had begun displaying symptoms of "runt puppy" syndrome. He was now beyond the cute puppy stage and was shaping into a rogue dog. If clothes were torn from the clothesline and dragged through the dusty yard, we immediately blamed Tige. If holes were dug in Mother's postage stamp lawn, we blamed Tige. If the garbage can was raided and bread wrappers, banana peels, and coffee grounds scattered outside the kitchen door, we blamed Tige. In general, Tige was aggressive, disobedient, and willful. He was also a coward. He chased the turkeys, but when an old gobbler ruffled his feathers, Tige tucked his tail and scurried to safety at the kitchen door. He dug into the hen yard. When the rooster in charge asserted his authority, Tige scrambled back through the compromised fence leaving bits of his fur dangling in wire.

Little Cricket's desire for a pair of cowboy boots did not wane. He showed Mother pictures of boots in the *Western Digest*. They were elaborately tooled and very costly. He pointed to the rack of boots on display at the feed and seed store. They were for big feet.

Anticipation of another Christmas hung in the air. Daddy, as he had on previous holidays, brought a pinon tree down from the high country. This time we decorated it with glass balls and strings of tinsel. A few gaudily wrapped gifts were tucked under its branches. Cricket eyed each with longing. He had no doubt that a pair of boots was in one of the enticing parcels.

On Christmas morning, a sturdy box covered with holiday foil contained exactly what he wanted, a pair of Justin Western Boots for Kids. Brown cowhide. Embellished with intricate leafs and curls framing the outspread prongs of a Texas longhorn. The rest of Christmas paled. Cricket had received his coveted boots.

Cowboy boots were designed with the horseman in mind to assure that his feet stayed in the stirrups. They had narrow toes, raised heels, and high arches. They were difficult to put on. Mule eared grips on the high shafts of the footwear allowed the cowboy to pull the stiff leather over his ankles. These very features made cowboy boots notoriously difficult to walk in.

Little Cricket not only walked in his cowboy boots, he slept in them. Through the day Cricket swaggered around The Ranch adding scuffed character to his boots. At night Mother wrestled the boots from him before she put him under the shower. Then the boots returned to his feet.

Cricket proudly rode Old Bill in true cowboy fashion, now. Day after day, Cricket, astride Old Bill, ambled around the back field, around the chicken coops, and down the dusty road to the mailbox, his feet dangling in Justin Boots.

Little Cricket returned Old Bill to the barn following a morning on the trail. He slipped off the horse, stepped onto the corral rungs, unbuckled the bridle and slung it over a fence post. He headed toward the house.

Bordering our property was an irrigation ditch. Often dry, on this day muddy water surged and swirled bank to bank. At intervals, rivulets were being channeled to rows of soybeans.

Cricket stopped to throw a rock into the water. He picked up a stick and tested the depth of the stream. Then, as things always seemed greener on the other side, Cricket wanted to get to the other side of the ditch.

He evaluated the situation. The ditch was not wide. He figured reaching the other side would not be a problem. He was, however, wearing his prized boots. Even at his tender age, Cricket knew those boots were made for riding, not for jumping. As a protective measure for his coveted footwear, he peeled the boots off of his feet. He hurled one boot across the stream. It teetered but landed safely on the opposite bank. Cricket picked up the other boot, lobbed it in the same direction. This boot also teetered, but, unfortunately, missed its mark, fell into the ditch, swirled along with the current, and then sank out of sight.

Armed with a stick, and encouraged by Tige who cocked his head curiously, Cricket poked and prodded the murky water. He tore at weeds and brambles as he vainly tried to locate his submerged boot. He scuttled along the ditch; his right foot sank in oozing mud; his left knee edged along the moist embankment. A few feet from the site of the mishap Cricket located his waterlogged boot. He pulled it out of the stream, cradled it like a cherished child, sobbed and laughed simultaneously. He pulled the dry boot over his muddy sock and limped to the house. Arrogant Tige loped jauntily beside him.

Cricket sidled into the kitchen where Mother was peeling vegetables for soup. How was he was going to explain the sodden footwear? His prized boot. Tige clawed at the door wanting to be part of the exchange.

Mother looked up from her task.

"Git!" she yelled at Tige, rebuking the dog for scratching the door. She turned to Cricket.

The drenched waif held his soaked treasure behind his back. Cricket glanced at the dog wagging his tail on the other side of the screen. Mother had not time to quiz him on his circumstances.

Little Cricket blubbered, "Tige pushed me."

New Boots

Chapter 18

THE SKY IS FALLING!

"You twerp!" I was addressing Cricket who had left the pasture gate open.

I ran along the east fence to the back of the field. The gate was one of those Texas gates – a wire contraption that was but an extension of the barbed wire fence – a flimsy but vicious construction. It lay in a jumbled heap just as Cricket had left it. I had to unsnarl the coils and then pull the section taut, stretch tangled wires to the corner post of the fence, then loop nooses, top and bottom, over the gate post. No easy feat even in good weather. It seemed like the ornery wires of the gate were not meant to fit the gaping hole in the fence.

Sunsets had been eerie for several evenings. Lingering tongues from El Sol's fiery breath outlined western mountains. Strata of sultry reds and petulant purples draped the skyline. The remainder of the firmament was gray.

Days, too, assumed lethargic dispositions. Occasionally the mood was punctuated by a capricious dust devil that skipped across the desert. Tumbleweeds scampered in the path of this mini-tornado.

We watched the sky, but life on The Ranch went on. Wash Day: I helped Mother guide loads of laundry through Water Witch. Sodden fabrics draped indolently on the clothesline and over the fence.

To the mailbox: I rode my bicycle to retrieve the mail.

The weather forecast in the newspaper (yesterday's *Republic*) indicated a storm moving in from Baja California. High winds. Rain.

Other chores: Mother and I checked each of the chicken houses. Starter mash to the new chicks. Grainier supplements to the growing pullets. Extra doses of calcium to the laying hens. We checked the drip spigots to make sure fresh water was filling their troughs. We dropped immunization doses into their water pans to ward off disease. By late afternoon Mother had taken a shower and was peeling potatoes for dinner.

Tumult struck. Act I was an entire choreography of dust devils performing maniac dervishes over the desert stage. They dipped and twirled. They curtsied and changed partners. Through some meteorological phenomena particles of dust and debris were picked up in spiraling vortex before they whirled backstage.

Mother ran out to the clothes line to rescue garments that thrashed and writhed in the swirling sand. I dashed about the house slamming windows and securing doors. Cricket was out on Old Bill. The lad was wise enough to turn back to the barn as a blanket of dust obscured the sun.

Cricket left Old Bill untethered behind the corral gate and darted to the house. But, apparently, when Cricket went out on his horseback ride, he left via a gate at the back of the pasture. He returned at the corral gate. The back gate had not been closed.

"Susan, run out and close the pasture gate!" Mother shouted.

So, there I was, struggling with ferocious barbed wires, rectifying yet another omission by my kid brother!

Act II. The fury of the storm hit as I tugged at the belligerent barbed wires. They coiled like boa constrictors with spines. Dust whipped around me. Grunting, I pegged the gate pole through the wire loop at the base of the fence post. I yanked the top of the gate, peeked at my progress through mere slits in my eyes, then threaded the top of the gate pole through the top noose of the fence post. Voila! The top wire loop of the fence post barely caught the gate post. At least it suggested that the gate was closed. Unless Old Bill knocked against the gate and jarred it from its precarious hook he would not wander away.

The relentless blizzard of dust enveloped everything in its path. My hair whirled like Medusa's. My teeth filled with grit. I could not see beyond my fingertips. Hand over fist, I groped my way back to Little House using the barbed wire fence as my guide.

Little House was taking a beating on its own. Dust crept under the doors, around the windows, through cracks and crevices that we did not know existed. A layer of silt carpeted the floor. We made foot tracks in the sand. Dust settled over tables, chairs, counter tops. It crept into the beds and infiltrated sheets and pillows. Powdery residue accumulated in pleats and ruffles of the curtains. We viewed the outside storm through a smothering veil.

Unsecured objects around The Ranch flailed about. Packing crates tumbled top over teakettle, some shattering as they crashed into objects in their path. Buckets, barrels, barrows, and tin siding toppled and whirled. Then almost as suddenly as the dust storm came upon us, it passed to create havoc upon other settlements in its wake. The curtain closed.

Act III. Crack! Boom! Kapow! Lightening cracked. Thunder roared. Electrical spears shot from heaven to earth. Some branched into brilliant webs and created panoply equaled only by July fireworks. The firmament opened. Rain cascaded in solid sheets.

Now water invaded Little House. Rain pelted windows and doors that faced the west. It trickled into Little House following the same paths as the sand. It drummed on the corrugated tin roof. It percolated through the ceiling. We dashed about setting pans and kettles under the leaks. Now we made splotchy foot tracks over the floor.

Through the evening Mother, Cricket, and I hovered in Little House while Rain God asserted his ill-tempered sovereignty. We seemed to be at the center of his tantrum. A final Crack! Little house rocked on her foundation. Lightning had struck a nearby power pole. Little House lit up like a

Christmas tree. Instantly it was as black as midnight. Electricity was out.

That last crescendo was the pinnacle of the storm. We crawled into our muddy beds. We were lulled by thunder growling as the storm moved eastward. Rain God tossed a lightening spear across the firmament, and the final curtain went down.

Next morning the ranch yard was a-tumble – broken branches, crumpled awnings, dented roofs, crushed troughs. First, we had to check the flocks to see how they weathered the storm. After all, the top half of the chicken houses was open wire. Sand and rain would have pelted the occupants. Predictably, a certain number had expired in the tempest and had to be dispatched to the incinerator. The survivors scratched about restless and agitated, their feathers still plastered to their ribs.

Wind and rain had slashed an arroyo across the front corner of our property. A small rivulet had formed at the bottom of the rift and was trickling under the fence and out to the road. In creating the gorge, water had cut through a gopher domicile. Its network of tunnels was compromised. While we examined the new geological feature of our property, a lethargic rattlesnake crawled out of the maze where he had taken shelter during the storm.

Wind, dust, rain, sun. Eternal elements. A blunt reminder of the ephemeral nature of our place under the sun.

A tenacious creosote bush grew by the front fence, a scrappy evergreen shrub. Its waxy resinous leaves were responsible for the odor punctuating the air, a peculiar acrid fragrance associated with rain upon a thirsty land. Twisted yellow petals bloomed on its bush for half of the year. After the creosote bloomed the flowers turned into small fuzzy white capsules that littered the ground. Native peoples, and later settlers in the West, used the plant as a virtual pharmacy. Inhaling steam from the leaves was said to relieve congestion. Medicinal tea brewed from its leaves was purported to cure everything from coughs to cancer.

The creosote bush had been partially uprooted in the

tempest. The improvised gully had cut through at the base of the plant. Roots of the creosote were now exposed as a small ravine evolved. Its major stem bent, the bush lurched toward the east.

Unearthed after eons, a cluster of pottery fragments dangled among the roots of the creosote – buff colored clay, decorated with reddish emblems suggesting thunderclouds, lightning bolts, and swirling eddies. Traces of another civilization lay beneath the sands of time. The Hohokam, prehistoric people who inhabited the desert centuries before "white-man" moved in, had been no strangers to summer squalls. Shards of an ancient vessel read like a diary of such experiences.

What would remain of our civilization in the desert when our time was done?

Chapter 19

IN MATTERS PRIVY

It was, indeed, a closet. But, "water closet" was a misnomer because water flowed sparingly through it. Water was liquid gold on The Ranch. When liquid did flow, pipes snarled like the hounds of Hades before they spit out a rusty stream laced with silt.

The "throne" in our water closet was positioned so that while I perched on the stool my knees pressed against the opposite wall. I sat gingerly with my weight thrown onto my left buttock. A critical split in the toilet seat threatened to pinch the right side of my rump if it rested on the rim.

The bathroom of our four-room domicile was a narrow thoroughfare between the Pahlah and the bedroom. The person on the throne commandeered entrances to both rooms. A locked door at either access simply frustrated family members passing through the house.

"Susan, I need to get to the bedroom," Mother snapped from the Pahlah side while she balanced a basket of laundry on her hip. Usually, I left the doors unlocked and let traffic flow.

On the wall across from the throne a Southwest Flour and Feed calendar pronounced the seasons. July's picture was a pastoral scene; black and white cows grazed placidly on emerald grass. A brook bisecting a meadow careened merrily over rocks and eddied along the banks.

Mother made notes on the calendar. "Ice Man." "Doctor

– Cricket." "Pullets – #2." These cryptic messages signified that 100 pounds of ice would replenish the melting sliver in the wooden ice chest; that Cricket had a doctor's appointment; that the chickens in coop #2 would be ready for market; the poultry broker would be wheeling his stake-bed truck into the yard to cart away crates of indignant fowl.

Much of my early education transpired on the "throne." I learned my numbers from 1-31. I learned to spell the days of the week as well as the months of the year. I learned the nights of the full moon. And, I learned that not all farms were situated in a drought-prone desert. August's calendar picture was a red barn; sleek horses whinnied over the side corral. September's picture was a covered bridge flanked by lush orchards ready for harvest.

One could, and indeed had to, attend all bathroom matters in half a pivot. A pitted sink hung on the wall next to the toilet. Mother shirred muslin feed sacks to make a skirt around the sink camouflaging a galvanized tin pail and scrub brushes below. I stood on a stool to brush my teeth. A watery eight-year-old reflection peered back from the flaking silvered glass. Four jelly glasses were lined on the window sill; each held a color-coded toothbrush. The one I used was green. I grimaced and preened. I crossed my eyes. I used an allotted half-glass of water to brush my teeth.

A moldy shower was tucked behind curtains of the self-same feed-sack variety as the sink. When engaged, the shower pipes chugged and gasped before waking the sleeping curs of hell. The pipes commenced to growl for the duration of a three-minute shower.

Mother's shower accoutrements were lined on a shelf over the pitted sink. A hair brush, a box of bobby pins, a tube of Yodora, and a can of Yardley's English Lavender. Following her afternoon ablution Mother dusted her nose with translucent powder, colored her lips with Cherries in the Snow and, alas, wilted like a soft tea cake.

My daily shower was more rudimentary. Before bedtime Mother sprayed my vital parts to the accompaniment of the yowling pipes, turned off the water, scoured me with a cake of

Ivory and a rough washcloth, recommenced the growling ensemble, and sprayed off the suds. She whisked me into pajamas and trundled me to bed.

As long as the well was working, our water closet was functional. But in desert regions, pumps failed, and wells went dry. When that happened we reverted to the facility beside the barn.

* * *

Unpainted, sun-bleached, in harmony with the environment. It was perched at the back of the ranch yard, behind a row of chicken coops, in line with the barn, and before the horse pasture began. It was a classic wooden shell, the door replete with the sign of a crescent moon. Daddy called it The Thunder Shed. Mother called it The Privy.

It was a cozy turn-around if you were inside. A bench-high box was hammered across the back wall. In the middle of the box was an oblong hole discreetly covered by a trap door. All of this was constructed over a six-foot-deep pit.

There were occasions we resorted to The Privy. If Daddy contacted Butch Brown's tanker service to bring water to The Ranch, he, for sure, would require us to trot out to The Privy when we had to relieve ourselves. Daddy would not let us waste five gallons of precious water flushing the toilet.

I always thought that The Privy was spooky. It was not maintained by the same standards as the facilities in the house. The door dangled loosely on rusty hinges. It screeched when I pulled it open.

I kicked the siding to urge any desert critters out of hiding – mice, ground squirrels, even snakes – heaven forbid! Cracks between the planks and knotholes in the boards provided daytime light and natural ventilation. Dust cascaded from the ceiling. The bench was splintered. I lifted the trap door covering the oval hole and peered into the netherworld to make sure creepy-crawlies would not caper over my exposed derriere.

Furnishings met the basest standard tolerable. Daddy

Long-Legs had strung tangled webs from corner to corner. Unfortunate flies and beetles were trapped in the arachnid curtains. A roll of toilet paper, stuck on a ten penny nail, trailed languidly to the floor. Dated reading material consisted of a pre-War Sears and Roebuck Catalog and the *Republic's* society page, six months old. A bucket of lime and a metal scoop were handy for when the appointment was over.

We did not generally have to worry about frosty rumps when we used the outdoor facilities. Most of our water problems occurred in the summertime. Summer in the Arizona desert did not bring a chill factor. It brought a drought factor.

May and June were hot and dry. Mid-July, and the thermometer registered triple digits. Water that we urged from the well was being used for animals and for our critical necessities. Without surplus water to irrigate, tufts of grass around the ranch buildings scorched and wilted. Leaves on the orange trees curled and dropped. Even hearty desert foliage stood dusty and dormant.

Summer storms offered a mixed blessing. Wrathful, ravaging, they also replenished the thirsty land. Monsoon – an improbable term in the desert, but common parlance – referred to an unpredictable mix of conditions bringing humid air and rain from the Pacific Ocean. Storms, preluded by severe winds and walls of dust, rolled in from the western coast of Mexico. Tree branches crashed to the ground. Unfettered property tumbled over the range.

During one such tempest the roof of The Privy was lifted and settled unceremoniously in the corral.

Fixing The Privy was low on Daddy's priorities. Other repairs were more urgent. Chicken coops to be mended, irate fowl to be settled, broken branches to be trimmed. And, most crucial of all, the well to be resurrected. Our pump suffered severe damage in the deluge. Repairing the pump was vital to our livelihood on The Ranch.

During those days of reassembling the rest of our property we resorted to the roofless privy. Mother made her way to the, now, very well ventilated outhouse. She assumed her position in the private hut. She reached for the Sears

Catalog and, undoubtedly, began compiling a wish list of household luxuries – a toaster that browned two pieces of bread on both sides at the same time; a carpet sweeper that actually picked up inevitable desert dust; and (Heaven forbid!) an electric refrigerator that had a freezer compartment big enough to make two trays of ice cubes. Mother was lost in a reverie of a pampered indulgence.

To the west of our property McElroy had cultivated a section of desert land and planted it in soybean. The crop thrived after the rain. Long parallel rows of bushy foliage faded into the horizon. A resurrected WWI biplane was at work over the field. It flew up and down the long rows dispensing insecticides over the crop.

The pilot looped gently over our ranch, over Mother perched in the aerated privy. He gave a gentlemanly nod and tipped his wings.

Box 7, Black Canyon Stage Route

Mother with Cricket age 3 and Susan age 6

Daddy in orange grove

Cowboy Cricket wearing his new boots

Susan and Cricket. The world was our playground

Susan and Cricket. The school bus dropped us at the gate.

Susan. Little House in background.

Chapter 20
CHICKEN ON SUNDAY

... and Monday ... and Tuesday ... and Wednesday.

Baked chicken, fried chicken, roasted chicken,
broiled chicken
Braised chicken, stewed chicken, barbecued
and boiled chicken

We had freshly slaughtered chicken in some form almost every day of the week. Gravied, souped, creamed, creoled, gumboed, bisqued. Mother mastered 101 ways to disguise the omnipresent chicken. Most frequently, Mother slit a young pullet in half, sprinkled it with salt and pepper, and slid it under the broiler. The chicken that we ate was butchered, bled, gutted, and plucked the day that we ate it.

The rest of our diet was more Spartan. It would be years before we acquired our first Kelvinator, an electric refrigerator that chilled our milk, crisped our vegetables, and held pieces of meat for several days without concern of spoilage. Meanwhile, we kept our few perishables in a wooden ice-box. Every Tuesday, the ice-man, making a round into ranch country, chunked a 100-pound frozen block into our oaken chest. Most of our victuals came from cans. Canned corn, canned carrots, canned spinach, canned tomatoes. And to vary our protein intake we had canned tuna, canned salmon, canned Spam,

Vienna sausage, and sardines. Mother bought a delicacy called pickled pigs feet for Daddy, but the rest of us politely declined that treat. So, although Mother was pretty inventive in the ways of chicken, the rest of her menu was rather mundane... canned peaches, canned pears, canned applesauce...

We had eggs in almost as many ways as we had chicken. Fried, scrambled, deviled, poached, scalloped, creamed, sautéed, omeletted, puddinged. When the hens were in a laying mode, Mother was known to throw an egg or two in the most unlikely recipes. She diced hard-boiled eggs into canned spinach or green beans. She whipped an egg into orange juice and created the rancher's version of an Orange Julius, a concoction created in franchise stands popping up across the nation.

Mother's classic sweet treat was a one-egg cake, a frugal recipe left over from depression era when eggs were a precious commodity. With our plethora of eggs, Mother cracked one egg, then another into the batter. She shrugged her shoulders, adding another egg, and yet another, to the mixture before pummeling the concoction with a wooden spoon. She poured the smooth egg-laced batter into a cast iron skillet and set it on a rack inside Butane Stove.

"Don't slam the door!" Mother admonished as cake and oven began a tenuous relationship.

If Butane Stove were in a benevolent mood, the oven radiated and the fragile cake batter lifted like a cloud then browned like a sun-baked mountain. If Butane Stove were aggravated, he took it out on the cake. The risen dome cratered in the middle and settled in striations like a bog.

Mother wasn't much of a cookie baker except at Christmas time. During the holidays she pulled out her recipe box and produced trays of classic treats – Christmas cutouts, gingerbread men, pinwheels, oatmeal, and chocolate chip. She brought platters of these cookies to school for our Christmas parties. We reveled in her once-a-year culinary extravaganza. But, generally, Mother thought cookies were a nuisance.

"Don't inhale your cookies!" Mother grumbled as Daddy popped a crunchy disk in his mouth and consumed it in a single wolfish gobble.

Mother made a special dessert when bananas from the market were on sale. She layered vanilla wafers, egg pudding, and soft bananas. The dish was pretty tasty on first serving, but left-over pudding that was scooped up on second-night slumped and wept, and the bananas turned a menacing black. I preferred the one (or two or three or four) egg cake even if it had sunk in the middle.

Nor did Mother make bread, at least not the plump yeasty variety that farm women have been noted for. She brought loaves of soft white bread home from market for our breakfast toast and sandwiches. Most of the time, my school sandwiches, made of doughy Wunderbread, were smashed and misshapen by the time I retrieved them from my lunch pail. The breads that Mother did make with some regularity were cornbread and baking powder biscuits. I preferred a slice of Spam nestled in a biscuit to sandwiches made of the wunder-stuff. There was a short period when bakers in the Phoenix-based Rainbo Bakery went on strike. There was no bread in the grocery stores. I lauded the baker's strike because Mother was forced to roll out biscuits and heat up the skillet for cornbread.

In spite of the fact we lived on a small spread, we were not conventional farmers. From our row of citrus trees, we had an abundance of grapefruit wedges, orange slices, and lemonade for half the year. Irregular water patterns prevented us from using that precious commodity to irrigate anything more. Besides, Mother was busy enough keeping the fowl in feather. She did not aspire to be hoeing corn or canning tomatoes.

Because we lived on the edge of a farm belt, we sometimes benefited from the bounty of the fields near us. When following a harvest wagon as it bounced along a rutted road, we recovered carrots or lettuce or potatoes or onions that fell off. Watermelon did not fare so well when they bounced off the wagons, but occasionally Romero delivered a couple of those splendid emerald melons, sweet and lush, from McElroy's field.

A burlap bag of dry pinto beans leaned against the back

wall of the pantry. Pinto beans and cornbread were almost as regular as chicken in our repertoire of meals. Mother sorted and washed four cups of beans. A few stones inevitably lurked among the beans, and these had to be removed before the cooking process began. If they weren't discovered before cooking, an unfortunate bite might crack a molar at dinnertime. Mother chopped an onion and added bacon grease. Salt and red chili gave the beans a lively zest.

Mother got out the pressure cooker, a Ward's twelve-pound cast-aluminum cylinder. Its domed lid was secured to the base by six clamps. A rubber gasket around the lid ensured a tight seal. Regulatory apparatus, pressure valves, and meters akin to cockpit paraphernalia, were lined across the top. This latent device rattled and danced on the top of Butane Stove. It spit and hissed. It chugged and steamed. The red needle on the pressure meter waved manically. The beans under pressure sounded like they were engaging in a war-dance.

One afternoon the ceremony erupted into a full-fledged war-path.

"Crack!"

"Pow!"

"Blam!"

We were under attack! The house trembled. We raced to the kitchen to discover that the pressure cooker bomb had detonated. It sailed to the ceiling then crashed to the kitchen floor. A circle of bean soup dripped from overhead. The rest of our dinner oozed across the floor.

Daddy clomped into the kitchen. He tossed his hat on top of the ice-box.

Sniff. Sniff. "Something smells good." Drops of bean soup landed on his head.

"What's for dinner?"

"Chicken!"

Mother handed Daddy the hatchet.

Chapter 21
TURKEY TROT

Chickens were our business; turkeys were but a sideline. Mother ordered a half-dozen turkey poults with an eye to having one for Thanksgiving and another for Christmas. They were nurtured through their infant stage along with the Leghorn chicks. Four of the six poults survived life with the chicks. Because they were Turks we dubbed them Sultan, Sheik, Abdul, and Omar. As they began to outstrip their chicken counterparts in size and in belligerence, they were separated and moved to a makeshift shelter under the tamarisk trees near the kitchen door. They came to be fed when they were called, and they came to be fed when they were not called. A gaggle of Turks surrounded us whenever we stepped out of the house. The gangly black birds abandoned any pretense of using the shelter and took up residence at the kitchen door. At night they settled companionably in the branches of the trees. They matured into ruffled fractious adults dividing themselves equally as toms and hens. Abdul and Omar became Abby and Ommy respectively.

Sultan and Sheik strutted and preened, gobbled and gawked. They spread great arcs of iridescent tail and flapped their crenulated wings. The wattles that fluttered under their beaks turned bright red when they were excited. Abby and Ommy clucked and scolded. They became fat and impudent on a diet of corn supplemented by bread scraps, grasshoppers, grubs, and lizards.

Thanksgiving neared. Mother planned her feast around Sultan. He was to be enhanced with cornbread dressing, gravy, mashed potatoes, candied yams, cranberry sauce, stuffed celery, and pumpkin pie.

The day of slaughter arrived. It was the day before our promised Thanksgiving feast. Throughout history societies have employed execution as a means of punishing criminals or suppressing political dissent. Decapitation, impalement, and dismemberment were among the heinous death sentences ordered by despotic rulers or vigilante committees to maintain order in a realm. Poor Sultan's fate was sealed as we added post-mortem hanging, drawing and quartering, boiling in oil, and slow-slicing to a litany of barbaric insults.

Mother postponed the macabre event in hopes that Daddy would be home in time to perform the execution. Hours passed. It became evident that Mother would have to attend to the bloody task herself.

"Your father certainly manages to be absent at the most convenient times."

I missed the sarcasm of her comment.

Mother pulled the ax from its hook in the shed. She took a handful of corn. A parade of unsuspecting turkeys followed her to the guillotine. Sultan hopped obligingly on the block fully expecting an additional share of kernels. From this vantage point he stood eye-to-eye with Mother. Sultan glared expectantly at Mother. He ruffled his beard. He shook his wattle. The warty skin on his head and throat turned from pasty blue to crimson, a sign that he was agitated. His companions scratched indolently at Mother's feet. Mother dropped the ax. In resignation, she threw the rest of the corn on the ground. Sultan flapped to the ground and joined his companions in their feast.

We ate chicken for Thanksgiving.

Nor did we have turkey for Christmas. Sultan strayed from the safety of the kitchen door one evening. He met his comeuppance in the form of a hungry coyote that drifted in from the range. All that remained was a flurry of feathers testifying to a brief battle for life and a dusted path where the coyote had dragged the arrogant bird into the desert. Mother could not find it in her heart to commit Sheik to the oven. We ate chicken for Christmas.

As nature would have it, in the spring Abby and Ommy began to lay eggs. At first we discovered eggs in widely distributed hideaways. Often they were broken, found first by a critter from the desert, a skunk or a coyote, or maybe even a snake. Abby and Ommy did not seem to have mothering instincts. At last, we collected a few tan speckled specimens and placed them in the thicket under the tamarisks. Submitting to nature's call, Abby and Ommy ruffled over their new charges, and, in time, an assortment of turklets pipped forth. Surely these nameless beings would provide a holiday meal. They grew in the nature of their parents. And now we had a dozen turkeys tousling at the kitchen door. We had to put metal bracelets around the legs of Abby, Ommy, and Sheik to distinguish them from their offspring.

By now Abby, Ommy, and Sheik were crusty old veterans, but their children were fattening up nicely. Daddy was committed to slaying the turkey this Thanksgiving. Mother had her eyes on one of the young gobblers that had outsized the others. She singled him out for Daddy.

After dinner Daddy honed the ax. Like a frontiersman, he sallied forth with steely resolve to provide food for the Thanksgiving table. Daddy would not fool with bits of corn to lead a bird to slaughter. He would grab the fowl by its feet, carry it to the chopping block, and off its head.

I stood at the kitchen sink drying dishes when the commotion began. Gobbles and squawks and angry clucks. Batting wings. Blasphemies. Daddy appeared at the kitchen door, his hair pasted to his forehead, his shirt unbuttoned and pulled from his pants. The ax dragged lamely at his side.

"Isn't anybody going to help me?" he sulked.

Turkey Trot

    We rallied forces in the brisk November evening. And, thus began a turkey trot. Turkeys scattered to the four corners of the ranch yard. Mother and Cricket and I took off after an errant bird, any bird. The first bird captured was carried in its squawking wretchedness to Daddy who wielded the ax, this time with masterful precision.
    We ate turkey for Thanksgiving.

Chapter 22

BLANK EGGS

A basket of wooden eggs sat on the kitchen window sill. They weren't left over decorations from the Easter Bunny. These smooth elliptical objects were for the sole purpose of duping our hens.

Mother had a dozen Rhode Island Red layers. From that flock we typically retrieved six or eight eggs a day. If the hens started to fall down on the job Mother would take some of the blanks from the basket and nestle them into the boxes in the hen house.

Mother's hens had to be coddled. If they weren't, they didn't produce. This meant no disturbance around the hen house. Mother didn't let us play in their vicinity. If a ball slammed against the wood siding, a flurry of mad hens squawked and flew into the side fenced pen. They bustled and argued and were generally discontent. Out of sorts meant no eggs.

These hens had to be fed properly. The basis of their diet was a laying mash consisting of grains and assorted vitamins. Calcium, in the form of ground-up oyster shells, assured that their egg shells would be strong.

The biddies expected privacy and security. Our hen house was furnished with a row of discreet straw-lined boxes where the hens were supposed to accomplish their egg-laying. Their tendency was to seek more secluded spots for their nesting sites. Their choices were somewhat limited in this 15 foot square domicile and its fenced side yard. But these wily hens were adroit in finding obscure corners and niches behind the feeding troughs to lay their eggs.

The laying team depended on good lighting. Long days meant long laying hours. Fortunately, in Arizona, we had plenty of sunshine. Mother did not have to trick her brood with false lights to suggest that the sun was up. But she did try to trick them with blank eggs.

The hens were contrary, stupid fowl. They were known to peck at the fragile objects that they produced. The counterfeit eggs were supposed to discourage the hens from destroying the delicate shells of the real thing. These phonies were also supposed to encourage the hens to establish their nests in the approved sites. A two-fer-one purpose.

I'm not sure if the fake eggs accomplished what they were supposed to. But they did serve another purpose. One summer night the hens were nestled in their designated boxes, feathers fluffed around real or imaginary eggs. We, too, had gone to bed along with the chickens. Evening solitude settled over the desert.

Not every creature was asleep in the nocturnal calm of a warm summer's eve. A diamondback rattler curled out of a gopher hole. He stretched languidly and began his search for nourishment. The unsuspecting hen house was in his path. He slithered along the desert floor making tell-tale s's in the sand. He came upon an open knothole in the coop and stuck his head through; his flickering tongue sensed the presence of live meat. The viper arched his back and wound his four foot length into the nesting box at the end. The resident hen sensed a disturbance and fluttered. The snake, in a reaction of defense, struck at the hen, impaling her with deadly fangs. The hen squawked and flapped wildly, alerting the rest of the coop to the impending danger before she succumbed to the poison. The other hens joined the fracas. Claws and feathers whirled while the inhabitants of the hen coop sought refuge on higher roosts.

The snake, undeterred by the ruckus he had caused, found what he was looking for. Eggs. The slithering serpent swallowed an egg whole, maybe two eggs. In his gluttony the thieving bastard swallowed one of the counterfeit plugs and crawled away.

The next morning we were greeted by mayhem in the henhouse, a dead biddy and her restless crones. It was several days before the hens returned to their safe and secure habits of producing eggs with or without the wooden blanks.

And even more time passed before we found the satanic culprit stretched out in the back field. Vultures had picked at his bones so that there was little left but his vertebral column and an undigested wooden egg.

Chapter 23

THIS LITTLE CHICK WENT TO MARKET

"Cleaners – Bill's coat; Penney's – elastic; Bashas' – corn meal, baking powder, bleach, starch… oh yes, coffee, peanut butter." Mother ticked off the items on her shopping list. "Cricket needs socks," she remembered. She added "socks" to her Penney's list.

We made Thursday afternoon pilgrimages to Glendale to replenish ranch supplies and to stock the kitchen larder. If Mother neglected to pick up pins for her sewing project she had to put them on her list for next week. Likewise, if she forgot mustard or pickles, we were doomed to eating dry sandwiches for a week. Generally Mother's shopping list was comprised of three parts.

First and foremost was a list of commodities for the chickens. We procured these from Southwest Flour and Feed, abbreviated to The Feed 'n Seed Store. Dietary essentials such as nutritionally enhanced mash for the chicks; grit, scratch and grain for the maturing pullets; oyster shell for the laying hens. Other items on her list for the flocks might include additional water pans, replacement spigots for watering troughs, Lysol for sterilizing empty chicken houses.

The second list was a grocery list, predictable and unimaginative. For this we stopped at Bashas'. Canned Spam, canned tuna, canned salmon, canned . . . peas, beans, corn, spinach, peaches, fruit cocktail. And, of course the staples that

Box 7, Black Canyon Stage Route

pulled a meal together – flour, shortening, sugar, coffee, syrup, baking soda. This list also included agents that kept home and body clean – Dutch Cleanser for the kitchen sink, Oxydol for the laundry, Ivory soap for the shower, Ipana toothpaste, and Breck shampoo.

Mother's third and sundry list took us to assorted stores on the square. New socks for Cricket, undershirts for Daddy, and pink thread for a dress she was making for me required us to go to J.C. Penney's. There a clerk procured the requested items, took Mother's money, and put cash and sales slip in a little can at the end of a long pulley-cord. Clerk gave the pulley a sharp yank, and the can whizzed along a wire to a cashier who sat in a mezzanine office overlooking the store. In time, a bell rang. The can zoomed back to Clerk who gave Mother a proper receipt for her purchase as well as the requisite change. I liked to go to Penney's, if only to watch financial transactions zip overhead from four points in the store.

Mother's sundry list might remind her to purchase a new ledger and pencils at Sprouse-Reitz 5¢ & 10¢ Store or to leave Daddy's boots at the cobbler's to be resoled.

Next we headed to the library. The Glendale Public Library hunkered in the middle of the town square. It was surrounded by thick grass, stately shade trees, and benches where old men collected to play checkers. The library was my favorite spot in the entire world. It was cool, dark, and quiet. I knew from the moment I stepped into the foyer that I had entered a place of reverence.

Mother returned a basket full of books that we had checked out the previous week. Cricket and I headed to the children's room, a special retreat lined with colorful volumes that captured the imagination. My goal had been to read every book in the room, and I began on the east wall with the first six books on the shelf. My resolve to read systematically through the books waned as books on other shelves beckoned. I finally succumbed to selecting my weekly allotment of books from the shelves at large. I learned of cultures around the world as I read my way through the *Twins Books* by Lucy Fitch Perkins: *The Dutch Twins, The Irish Twins, The Mexican Twins, The Puritan*

Twins. One book from that series was later pulled from the library shelves because it was considered socially insensitive: The *Picaninny Twins*. Other books that formed my childhood reading pleasure also found themselves on banned or censored lists: *Little Black Sambo, Gulliver's Travels, Huckleberry Finn*. I devoured the *Little House* series by Laura Ingalls Wilder, and then moved on to the *Nancy Drew Mystery Books*. One day Mrs. Teague introduced me to the "Adult" side of the library. Until then I thought one had to be a card-carrying grown-up to browse those aisles. She showed me the series of *Jalna* books. My horizons expanded. The reading world of adults as well as children was at my fingertips.

We proceeded to the Ryan-Evans Drug Store where Mother presented Cricket's prescriptions to be refilled, ointments and elixirs that quelled his insufferable allergies. As we waited for the remedies, we sat at the fountain and ordered supper from a limited menu. Even as a child, I was a person of predictable routine.

"I'll have a ham sandwich and a small coke." I closed the menu after appearing to ponder the choices.

We packed a week's worth of errands into Thursday afternoons. From the pharmacy we descended upon Miss Emma Treadwell, piano teacher *par excellence*. Trained at the Boston Conservatory of Music, she spent her days drilling scales into ten-thumbed cretins.

Cricket and I, and then Mother, took half-hour turns under her tutelage. Mother was her only grown-up student, unless you counted Natasha Cannova who was already in college and had taken lessons from Miss Treadwell for twelve years.

Mother longed to learn how to play the piano. She began with rudimentary Thompson books just like Cricket and me. At home, after the supper dishes were put away, Mother pulled up to the discordant Howard upright and hammered out her cords and scales. Eventually, Mother progressed to simplified compositions of "Nola" and "Deep Purple." Her repertoire was a bit more refined than the ditties that Cricket and I played.

The highlight of Thursday was going to the movies.

Thursday night was bank night at the El Rey Theater, so the cinema was always packed. For fifty-five cents Mother purchased an adult ticket and two kiddy fares to the movie of the week. On bank night, our ticket stubs were thrown into a wire basket, and we had a chance at winning the weekly jackpot.

We thrilled to a succession of cowboys and comedies, dramas and spoofs. *West of the Alamo, The Blue Dolphin, The Best Years of Our Lives, Strangler in the Swamp*. We giggled at *Mickey Mouse* and *Bugs Bunny* as cartoons cavorted over the screen. We watched the news reels as a Cold War rose up in the wake of a hot war, as UFO's landed in Roswell, as Polio raged and a vaccine was sought.

The ticket basket whirled to a stop and a child selected from the audience pulled out a stub.

"0783!" the theater manager cried.

Mother groaned. 0784 was her number.

Week after week we gripped our ticket stubs to see if one of us was the lucky winner of a $25 jackpot. A succession of gleeful recipients paraded on stage, but in all of our Thursday nights at the El Rey, we only clutched our tickets and remained ever hopeful.

Late Thursday evening we pulled into The Ranch yard. Cricket always fell asleep on the way home, and Mother had to carry him to his bed and tuck him in for the night.

Chapter 24
THE PEDDLER'S WAGON

"We have a new product for spring." The Fuller Brush Man shook a fluffy red dust mop in Mother's face. "Its swivel head permits you to reach into far corners of the room. It captures every lost dust mouse under your bed." He demonstrated by running the mop behind the piano and retrieving a feathery bouquet of dust tendrils.

Anything we missed on market day we did without until next week. That was why the occasional peddler who ventured onto The Ranch aroused our yearnings and stood a good chance of tapping into Mother's pocketbook.

Mr. Fuller Brush was a roly-poly gnome whose graying mustache resembled the bottle brushes he sold. Twice a year his dented green wagon bounced through the gate. We watched as he dislodged himself from behind the steering wheel. He smoothed his wrinkled pants, slipped into a threadbare suit coat, and tweaked his bow-tie. Even on the outskirts of civilization Mr. Fuller Brush aimed to make a professional appearance. Through the dusty car windows we could see a forest of mop and broom handles. Mother was a sure-fire customer for Mr. Fuller Brush because she was always seeking a miracle tool to keep grime at bay.

It was early spring. The desert had responded to precipitation of winter (all three inches of rainfall). The hardpan desert floor snuggled under a yellow carpet of Desert

Marigold punctuated by tufts of Brittlebush. Thorny cacti adorned themselves with waxy crowns of white (the stately saguaro), or orange (the barrel cactus) or yellow (the fierce cholla). With the desert beautifying its act, Mother was inspired to beautify her man-made environs.

Naturally Mother wanted all the help she could get to rid the house of dust critters, so she purchased the miracle mop along with a scrub brush for the floor, a quart of furniture polish, and a new push broom for sweeping the chicken houses. Mr. Fuller Brush, pleased with his commission, took his leave. "I'll be back come fall!" And he rattled to the next ranch house due for spring cleaning.

One summer day an encyclopaedia salesman staggered in. The glories of spring had evaporated, and The Ranch scorched under the glower of El Sol. Dogs sought shelter in dusty pockets under the tamarisks. Chickens scratched lazily behind their wire enclosures. We squinted into the sun, and witnessed an ailing contrivance shimmy through the gate. A DeSoto coupe lurched to a stop by the garage. Smoke boiled from under its bonnet. In mid-July Mr. Encyclopaedia was making his way from Albuquerque, hoping to find lucrative sales in the greener pastures of Phoenix. He was stuck until his car cooled down. Undaunted by motor misfortune, he pulled out Volume I of the *Encyclopaedia Britannica* and began a loquacious spiel.

"Madam, I bring knowledge to you and to your children. The wisdom of the world is captured within these volumes." He flipped to a map of Africa. Subsequent pages pictured exotic creatures of the Dark Continent, giraffes, elephants, rhinoceroses, lions. Further scrutiny revealed fierce Zulu tribesmen clad in grass skirts and brandishing spears.

"Your children will learn the workings of the human temple." We gawked at celluloid overlays of the human body, the bones, the muscles, the blood system, the digestive track, and the internal organs.

"They will learn of creatures past." He pulled out Volume IV and pointed to dinosaurs of yore.

Mr. Encyclopaedia invited us to choose a subject we

wanted to know more about. Little Cricket piped up, "Horses!" and in Volume VIII we saw a parade of horses that included the Clydesdale, the Belgian Drafter, the Percheron, the Morgan, breeds that we were unlikely to encounter in our part of the West.

"For only a few cents a week you can provide your children with the equivalent of a college education!"

And Mother was hooked. She signed an agreement to purchase the newest edition, 24 volumes, of *Encyclopaedia Britannica*. In turn, Mother would save her egg money and send monthly payments to the distribution company.

An added bonus to this scholastic investment was a set of *Childcraft Books*, fourteen volumes of children's literature bound in bright orange covers. After the books arrived, The *Encyclopaedia Britannica* and *Childcraft* occupied places of prominence in The Pahlah. They were the source of many a school report, and they settled frequent dinner-time arguments. Mother or Daddy would decree, "Let's check the *Britannica*."

An itinerant Bible salesman appealed to Mother's conscience over our hit-and-miss Sunday School attendance record. Mother ordered a ten-pound family tome illustrated with Rembrandt's religious pictures. It was lavishly scrolled in gold leaf, *The Sermon on the Mount* immortalized on thin illuminated pages. Mother promptly began genealogy records on the fore pages starting with her and Daddy. I suppose Mother envisioned a long list of progeny added to the chart. As far as I know, the pedigree on those pages ended with Cricket and me. The Bible wasn't referred to as often as the encyclopaedia. It became a repository of curled photographs, school dance programs, and recipes for corn chowder. It was a good booster chair at the dinner table. Mother draped a towel over it, and little Cricket's skinny bottom kept it dusted.

Butane Man came occasionally. Our butane tank was a steel bomb permanently affixed on risers imbedded into the ground. Mother admonished Cricket and me to stay away from the tank fearing possible malfunction, leakage, or worse. However its round smooth sides beckoned impudent children. And on venturesome mornings Cricket and I scaled up the

Box 7, Black Canyon Stage Route

risers and straddled the casing. To us, this silver shell was a stagecoach, an airplane, or even a rocket to the moon.

In addition to feeding Butane Stove, our tank also piped combustible fuel to hazardous space heaters stretched across The Pahlah, the bedroom, and the bathroom. When the gauge read "LOW" Mother ordered fuel on our next trip to Glendale.

Clyde Aaron delivered gas to us in a butane tanker. He pulled a trademark cap over one eye. Clyde was bow-legged and sported Levis which sagged lamely over his skinny butt. A corpulent gut draped over his belt, rather like an apple set upon toothpicks. Clyde's uniform shirt puckered at each button as it tried to hold his stomach in check. Clyde was jolly, chatty, affable. He was also the father of a boy in my class. I was curious to see how other fathers made a living for their families. Clyde leaned languidly against the truck holding a long hose while gas funneled into the holding tank.

Ice Man came most frequently of all. We knew him as Rolf. He sidled in bearing frozen blocks clutched in the vise grip of ice tongs. Generally Mother ordered 100 pounds of ice once a week. However, during the dog days of summer, she upped her order to twice a week. Mother was generous chipping shards of ice for her afternoon tea. Rolf was tall, skinny, shifty-eyed, and disagreeable. He wore the classic white uniform of the ice man; however it was rumpled and soiled. It appeared unchanged from one delivery to the next. More than once Mother suspected that the ice Rolf put in our box was not a full 100-pound block. "Do you want to weigh it?" he growled, if questioned.

If we doubted the integrity of Ice Man, so did our dog, Betty. Betty was an otherwise amiable mutt. Her barks alerted us to disturbances on the ranch. She let us know when visitors entered the gate. But after she achieved our attention, Betty considered her vigilance complete, and she simply watched in rapt attention and wagged her tail. Not so with Ice Man. Betty's hackles rose the moment the ice wagon pulled through gate. She growled and snarled the duration of the delivery. Ice Man snarled back and kicked at our little white dog. No love was lost between Ice Man and beast.

Probably, the best peddler of all was Jingle Man. On summer Sunday afternoons we heard his ice-cream truck tinkling down the road. His calliope rendition of "Mary Had a Little Lamb," incessantly repeated, heralded his arrival. He made Sunday wages by driving into farm labor camps and selling frozen confections to weary workers. As he neared our ranch we begged Mother for money to buy Popsicles. Mother complained about Jingle Man's prices. He charged twice as much for his treats as did the grocer. We paid a nickel for an ice-cream bar at Bashas'. We paid a dime for the same product at the Jingle Wagon.

Nevertheless, the lure of a cool sweet treat triumphed over parsimony, and Mother usually raided the egg money to procure icy delights for the family. We lingered over Jingle Man's chests packed with "dry ice" and agonized over whether to indulge in a cherry Popsicle, an ice cream bar, or an Eskimo Pie.

Chapter 25

ONE OF US

"No, I cain't give you a refund on them bottles. I only give refunds on what's bought here! I never seen you before!"

Before we stepped inside Hersch's Last Chance Market a ragged woman pulled a little boy out the door. She settled him in a rusty wagon along with her meager purchases and a canvas water bag. She tucked a few empty soda bottles in the back of the wagon and trudged away.

"That woman tried to get a refund on them sody bottles," Mrs. Hersch huffed. "Didn't even buy the sody from me." Mrs. Hersch sought commiseration. "I cain't give money back on bottles to anyone what walks in the door. Never seen her before. Have you?"

Hersch's Last Chance was the closest we had to a corner market, and it was five miles from The Ranch. On weekly trips to Glendale we stocked up on tinned meat and vegetables, baking supplies, and a few items of fresh produce. Our larder replenished, we were usually set for the week. Only under dire circumstances did we venture in to Hersch's.

A weathered shack leaned at the corner where a wide canal crossed the Black Canyon Stage Route. Parking was limited to two dusty spaces in front of a listing porch. A hand lettered sign over the door identified the establishment as Hersch's, the last chance to buy groceries before you reached New River.

You didn't have to enter the premises to know that the place thrived on neglect. Crates of empty soda bottles were stacked haphazardly outside the front door. A bin of culled cantaloupe invited swarms of fruit flies. Shreds of faded newspaper, waxed bread wrappings, and crumpled candy bar wrappers drifted across the porch and lodged in the weedy landscape. A pile of dog-doo, conspicuously ignored, had plopped where paying customers had to watch where they stepped.

Inside was no more inviting. Dusty high windows let in a modicum of light. Splintery shelves lined the small, square room. A few cans of tomatoes, peas, corn, hominy, and lima beans comprised a selection of tinned vegetables. Peaches and fruit cocktail were the fruit cans of choice. Souring milk, butter, and cottage cheese were housed in a top-opening refrigerator box. Mold was growing on its wooden floor. A rack of squashed Wunderbread was by the front door. There were a few sacks of sugar, weevily flour, and miscellaneous condiments. Oxydol, Fels-Naptha and Ivory along with a few tubes of Pepsodent were the selections for general cleanliness.

Catering to its predominately Mexican field-hand clientele, Hersch's provided a good supply of beans, rice, masa, chilis, and corn husks for tamales. Coils of tripe (intestines of farm animals) were available for purchase to make menudo, a spicy stew that was purported to cure hangovers. And contributing toward the hangovers Hersch's displayed a wall of cervezas – Budweiser, Lucky Lager, and A-1 Pilsner beer. Another wall was lined with Thunderbird Wine and Night Train Express. Daddy said these gut-wrenching hooches tasted like diesel fuel laced with antifreeze. They were responsible for many a brawl outside Hersch's.

Mrs. Hersch sat like a bull-dog Buddha on a stool behind the cash register. A tier of stomachs cascaded under a tier of chins. She guarded the soda pop cooler stocked with bottles of Orange Crush, Nehi Strawberry, and Barq's Root Beer. Her jowls waddled, and a curtain of underarm avoirdupois waved when she struck out at the finger of anyone attempting to snitch peppermints, gumballs, or horehound from a row of jars on the counter. Penny candy, as well as everything else in Hersch's was appreciably more expensive than like-items were in town.

This day Mother needed something badly enough to stop at Hersch's. As we got out of the truck we had heard Mrs. Hersch's querulous voice yammering about "them sody bottles."

Mother purchased her needed item, although the urgency of it had waned. We drove away from Hersch's saddened and perplexed. The would-be soda bottle recycler and her load were not far down the road when Mother pulled our pickup alongside her.

"Where are you going?" Mother called out.

"That-a-way," the woman answered.

We were also going that-a-way and couldn't imagine the destination of this weary woman and unkempt child.

"Let me take you," Mother offered.

Gratefully, the woman accepted Mother's kindness. We lifted the wagon and parcels into the bed of our pickup. Cricket and I scrunched to the center of the bench seat to make room for our passengers.

Maddy and Jed were their names. Maddy settled wearily next to the window. She held Jed in her lap. An attempt at a smile revealed a mouth of crooked teeth. Stringy gray hair was pulled into a bun but tendrils drifted wildly from a net that attempted to contain them. Her dress was soiled, her shoes worn. Brown cotton stockings draped around her ankles.

Hollow-eyed Jed rested his head on her shoulder. He might have been five, a little younger than my brother. He was attired in a cotton t-shirt, too dirty to determine its original color. Denim overalls buttoned over his scrawny shoulders. Ragged tennis shoes flapped on his feet, much too big, no socks. His skinny ankles were crusty with grime.

Mother drove on. She attempted small talk with Maddy.

"Where do you live?"

"Up the road a ways. In the desert."

"How long have you been there?"

"A while."

"Is this your boy?"

"My grandson."

We drove past sections of irrigated cotton fields. We drove past McElroy's acres planted in soybean.

We drove past the road leading to a string of dry rancheros including our own.

Now raw desert stretched before us.

"Thar it is. Turn here."

Mother steered the pickup onto a dusty trail.

Hidden from the primary road, nestled under shedding mesquite trees, was a camp tent. A few upturned boxes provided seating and work space. A sooty fire pit was the center for meal preparation.

A snarling cur greeted us. He lunged toward us, his jaws snapping.

"Git!" Maddy struck out at the mongrel. He slunk to the sidelines but continued to growl.

This was Maddy's home. She had mysteriously appeared and set up camp miles from civilization. She was caring for a dirty little boy and a vicious dog.

In subsequent weeks Maddy became a part of our lives. Mother drove out to Maddy's camp.

"Here's a watermelon." Mother presented Maddy with a giant melon from McElroy's packing shed. On each visit Mother exchanged cans filled with clean water with Maddy's empty cans.

Mother was haunted by Maddy. "The desert wrings spirit from the soul," she muttered.

Mother attributed Maddy's bleak existence to the arid land. I think that Mother had always harbored a fear that the desert would eventually extract strength from her own soul. Her happenstance encounter with Maddy tapped into the well of her anxiety.

One morning I rode with Mother out to Maddy's camp. The tent was gone. A few tin cans rattled over the desert floor. The fire had been doused and only soot remained in its circular pit. As mysteriously as Maddy had appeared she was gone.

We happened to stop at Hersch's Last Chance later that summer.

Mrs. Hersch maintained vigil over the soda pop and gumballs just as we had left her weeks before.

"Don't see much of you folks," was her petulant greeting. "Wonder what happened to that old woman and that scraggly kid. Good thing I didn't give her a refund on them sody bottles. Never did come back. I could tell she warn't one of us."

Chapter 26

SAGUARO VILLAGE

"Location. Location. Location." The mantra of real estate agents.

The stately saguaro cactus standing at The Ranch gate was prime location for the apartment house of a host of desert birds. Its basic architecture consisted of a thick trunk and two giant arms that rose as corridors toward the sky.

Construction on Saguaro Village was begun by little Gila Woodpecker. The bright red cap on top of his head identified this laborer. The tool of his trade was a long pointed beak that withstood incessant hammering. He drilled and bored until he pierced the thick rind of the saguaro and refined the hollow. The resultant cavity was a safe place to set up housekeeping and raise a family. His children took after the old man. They had brown faces, black and white zebra-striped backs, and white wing patches that were visible when they became airborne. Next year Gila Woodpecker would not return to the old flat. He would set his sights on a new locale and start over. He left a trail of vacated apartments in the saguaro cactus for other birds to assume rent-free.

A Western Screech Owl was first to take up residence in one of the vacated flats. He slept during the day and came out at twilight to perch on the roof of Saguaro Village. He was a small ruffled grey bird distinguished by intense yellow eyes and feather tufts on his head. His primary call was a series of short whistles, "hoo-hoo-hoo," increasing in tempo and ending in a long trill. Keen night-time vision and excellent hearing enabled him to swoop quietly over his prey. His midnight meal was preferably small rodents, but he might consume a scorpion or perhaps a toad.

The Elf Owl was another permanent resident of Saguaro Village. We did not often see this sparrow-sized ghost. We were more likely to hear his high-pitched yipping cry, "whi-whi-whi-whi-whi-whi," as he darted out at night to catch bugs.

Eventually, other birds moved in and out of Saguaro Village. They, conventionally, might make their homes in tree branches, rocky ledges, or barn eaves, but the ready-made shelter of a saguaro cactus apartment was appealing to hawks, flycatchers, martins, finches, and even doves. They outfitted their rooms in the décor of their choosing. A diverse world of birds nested, fed, squabbled, and spied among themselves.

When the Brown-headed Cowbird took up residence in Saguaro Village the other birds shook their heads and twittered, "There goes the neighborhood." In days when Buffalo roamed the prairies, Cowbird moved along with him. Cowbird sat on Buffalo's back and conveniently pecked the fleas and insects imbedded in his shaggy coat. Because Buffalo was always on the move, Cowbird could not establish a home. Instead, Cowbird smuggled her eggs into the nests of other birds along the way. The eggs were cared-for and hatched by an unsuspecting surrogate mother. Young Cowbirds were greedy vociferous beggars, often usurping food from the natural children of the nest. Brown-headed Cowbird had not changed her nesting habits even though Buffalo no longer roamed the prairie. With the introduction of livestock to the West, Cowbird widened her range and found new hosts, but she continued her despicable practice of leaving her eggs for other mothers to hatch.

Mourning Doves were attracted to McElroy's alfalfa field across the road from us, and they assembled in droves. They waddled onto our land and scavenged seeds and waste grains they found between our buildings.

Mama Mourning Dove was only too happy to find

housing at Saguaro Village. Only she did not appropriate one of the hidey-hole apartments. She chose a prickly outside ledge where a giant arm of the cactus branched from the main column. She puttered about, carrying odd twigs and bits of grass onto her elevated niche then considered her nest building done. The resulting nest looked as if it might be blown away by a whisper. There Mama Dove would lay two eggs. The helpless hatchlings, called squabs, depended on Mama Dove for sustenance for their two-week fledgling period. Mama Dove might not have been a tidy nest builder, but she was actually a devoted mother. She rarely left her clutch unattended, but if she was flushed from her home for some reason, she assumed a broken-wing display and fluttered on the ground to distract predators from her young.

Mama Dove was a plump, soft, grey bird. Her plumage tended toward the iridescent. She had a small tidy head and a long tapered tail. Her plaintive call suggested a bird in despair, "ooAAH-cooo-coo-coo." However, when large numbers of doves gathered they assumed a raucous twitter that sounded like "too-late, too-late, too-late."

The saguaro was by no means the only cactus to provide asylum for birds. Cholla Court was residence for birds that preferred to live closer to the ground. Along our eastern fence several Teddy Bear Cholla interlaced with barbed wire like ivy twining on a trellis. From a distance this plant looked deceptively innocent, like fabric cosseting a soft, cuddly Teddy Bear. These chollas were constructed of sausage-like links covered with ethereal silver spines, which were actually hellacious thorns. Joints broke off from the larger arrangement and scattered over the ground. A segment took root and a new cholla was born. Getting into Cholla Court was more difficult than getting into a gated community, and many birds availed themselves of its protection.

Nestled in the thickest part of the cholla hedge, a Cactus Wren made her home. Her nest was a football-shaped structure made of grass, twigs, dead leaves, and lined with feathers. Cactus Wren's mate helped her construct this nest as well as five or six secondary nests in close proximity. The female

Cactus Wren chose the coziest of the lot for her brood, and the other nests served as decoys to confuse predators.

Cactus Wren touted the distinction of being the state bird of Arizona. She had a white belly with brown spots, black feathers on her throat, and speckled brown, black, and white feathers over the rest of her body. She was a noisy bird who communicated in a raucous vocabulary of "chuk-chuk, scri, tek, tzip." Inquisitive Tige, unlike his prudent mother, Betty, was compelled to explore the environs of Mother Cactus Wren. Cactus Wren, in turn, employed her long pointed beak, long legs, and long tail in dive-bombing the audacious dog. He scurried away from her domain chastised and whimpering.

On spring mornings Mama Quail scuttled under the citrus trees. She looked as if she were going to a party wearing a gray ball gown with russet sides laced in white. Her black face was carefully outlined with white mascara. She finished her ensemble with a distinctive plume atop her head. "Ka-KAA-ka-ka." Mama Quail had a plump breast, short legs, and roundish wings much like our chickens. She led a covey of little quail, six or eight, in parade formation. Her nest, also, was located on the ground floor of Cholla Court. If she were alarmed, she garnered her brood and sprinted into the undergrowth rather than taking flight.

Warner Brothers got it right when they created a cartoon character modeled after the Roadrunner. *Wile E. Coyote vs. the Roadrunner* was a parody on cat and mouse cartoons. We were as entertained by the awkward bird racing farm trucks down the road as we were by the comedian of cinema propelling across the movie screen.

Wild and lawless, Roadrunner was a vagabond of the desert. A member of the cuckoo family, he was tail-heavy and awkward; his beak was longer than his head. He wore scruffy black-brown-and-white mottled plumage. Beneath his bristle-tipped top-knot he appeared wide-eyed and startled.

Known for running across the desert, Roadrunner had long legs and strong feet. If he became agitated he was able to fly a short distance, but his stubby wings failed to keep his heavy body airborne for long. Roadrunner was particularly welcome around The Ranch because of his predatory predilections. He fed on some of the very critters that we wanted to be rid of – grasshoppers, caterpillars, rodents, scorpions, and snakes. Roadrunner was one of the few animals that actually went after smaller rattlesnakes. He used his wings as a blind, and then snapped up a coiled rattler by the tail. He cracked the snake like a whip then slammed its head on the ground. With his strong, sharp beak, he proceeded to deliver stab after stab at the base of the reptile's brain. In a disgusting climax, Roadrunner swallowed his prey whole. However, he was unable to devour the entire snake at one time, so he went about his business with a portion of the snake dangling from his beak. Inch by inch, the rattlesnake was gradually digested.

Mother hung a tube of colored nectar outside the kitchen window. It attracted hummingbirds. As we sat at the breakfast table we watched the amazing aerial acrobatics of Hummingbird. She could fly up, down, forward, backward, and sideways. She could even stop in midair. When the tiny iridescent bird was not sipping from our sweet nectar cylinder she was hovering above cactus blossoms or palo verde flowers. Hummingbird nested and raised her young in a palo verde tree near the house.

On the opposite end of the scale of birds, apart from tiny, fast, beautiful, nectar-eating Hummingbird, was Turkey Vulture. We usually called him Buzzard. He soared overhead gradually circling to earth to claim a road kill or a young calf that died in the desert. Often several vultures were part of a synchronized ballet. While soaring, Turkey Vulture held his wings in a V-shape and tipped from side to side taking advantage of perpetual updrafts of air. He made a slow, even graceful, descent. On the ground he had an ungainly gait. It required great effort for him to take flight again. He hopped, flapped his wings, and pushed off with awkward adieu.

Turkey Vulture had a head like that of his namesake, red, bald, and warty. Apparently, the bald head served an important purpose. Since the vulture's diet was carrion, he stuck his head inside rotting carcasses to retrieve his dinner. After dinner he was able to simply shake his head discharging sticky particles that clung to his bald scalp. The eerie presence of Turkey Vulture in the sky always brought to mind death and carnage.

Many birds I could not identify. However, one commoner was known to all. Mockingbird. Early morning he began warbling outside the window imitating yodels, pips, screetches, kaas, hoos, and moans of all the birds around him. His repertoire included the scriiiitch of the corral gate, the bark of the dog, and even the cluck-cluck of our hens

"What time is it? This is worse than the roosters!"

I pulled a pillow over my ears for I yearned for a few more winks. But, Mockingbird was serious about his task of arousing the world. He mixed a series of ripples and trills into his serenade and ended the interlude in a grand arpeggio.

"Aw shucks!" I threw back the covers. Sleep was impossible.

Chapter 27

CHICKEN LINEN

"Uh-oh!" I looked in dismay at the ragged dip in my hem line.

Hot September morning, but still early. The day after Labor Day. As I swung around the crooked gate post, the bottom of my skirt snagged on the rough wood. I scuffed my polished brown oxfords and got bullheads tangled in my yellow socks. I would be a sorry sight on the first day of school.

I had started out scrubbed, starched, and newly outfitted. A passing observer might have noted that, as I dashed out of the house, my attire bore an uncanny resemblance to Mother's curtains, for the self-same fabric fluttered over the kitchen windows. This was my prettiest new school dress. It was buttercup yellow. Tiny blue cornflowers danced over the fabric. It had a pleated bodice, a Peter Pan collar fringed in blue rick rack, and a sash that tied in a neat bow in back. Best of all, my dress had two big patch pockets on the skirt. My milk money, knotted securely in a handkerchief, was in one of the pockets.

My garment was the product of feed sacks from Southwest Flour and Feed. It was the result of weeks of careful shopping at the ranch supply store. Chicken feed and other grains were sacked in 100-pound textile bags. On our weekly visits to buy corn, seed, and mash for the chickens, we carefully surveyed the veritable hodge-podge of prints that encased the nutrients.

Mr. Grundy looked on with consternation, for he was afraid that he would be called on to retrieve a heavy sack buried at the bottom of the pile to match or complement Mother's ongoing stitchery project. I always wondered why he piled the bags so helter-skelter and did not organize them properly by fabric pattern. Choosing a feed sack was like selecting a gown for the prom. There were always many choices, but our budget generally allowed us to select but one at a time.

Sometimes, if a particularly pretty pattern caught Mother's eye she'd splurge. "I don't need the feed right now, but I'll take three bags of mash." Then she was assured of having enough fabric for a dress. Using this method, Mother had acquired enough of the cheerful yellow fabric to make not only curtains for her kitchen but a school dress for me.

A new dress from a feed sack involved a process. After Mother selected the bag, Mr. Grundy heaved it into the bed of our pickup. It rattled over washboard roads to The Ranch. Then it was stored in the barn along with other bags of nourishment for our poultry. It depended on the substance in the bag how long it took the chickens to consume it. Regardless, we went through a lot of bags of chicken feed.

When a feed sack was empty, Mother turned it inside out and shook the remaining crumbs and dust into the air. With her sewing snippers and a straight pin, Mother carefully pulled the commercial stitching so that, when opened, a square of fabric ensued. Many bags were engineered so that by pulling a single string the entire line of stitchery could be undone in one zip. What remained was a piece of cloth approximately 37 inches by 43 inches, equal to more than one yard of fabric. Three sacks were usually enough to make a dress.

The fabric was soaked so that the paper label would peel off. And then the feed sack was thrown into Water Witch where it swirled in colorful confetti with other sacks destined to be sewn into dresses, blouses, aprons, table covers, or curtains.

The sacks were pinned on the clothesline, an array of florals, stripes, fruits, checks, and vivid geometric designs.

Every whimsy imaginable fluttered in the breeze. When they dried, Mother ironed the fabric squares, folded them, and then stacked them on a citrus crate shelf where they waited until enough pieces came through the laundry to make whatever bit of finery was next on her project agenda.

No one in the family was exempt from feed-sack attire. Mother made clothes for herself. Several "ranch dresses" were pegged on the back of the bedroom door. These garments she wore as she did chores about The Ranch. They were faded and frayed. A sleeve might have ripped, or a button popped. Mother also had a row of feed sack "town dresses" hanging on a rod in the closet. These were crisply starched garments that she donned when she went to market or to PTA meetings. One holiday when Mother brought cupcakes to my school party she wore a new novelty "chicken linen" dress. The print featured gay little Christmas wreaths with red bows.

Mother made shirts and pajamas for Cricket and even shirts for Daddy. Daddy might wear Mother's home-made shirts while he mucked the chicken coops, but I noticed when he went to work on his other job, he donned starched store-bought chambrays or khaki work shirts.

Besides the colorful print sacks that were the fabric of dresses and play clothes, there were unbleached muslin sacks, the basis of petticoats, panties, and night gowns. Before unbleached muslin bags could be made into garments they had to be soaked and sun-bleached to remove tell-tale logos from the fabric. Many times a faint, but distinct, *Red Star,* the product of Hayden Flour Mill, was visible across my rump while I swung from the monkey bars on the school playground.

Tightly woven unbleached muslin "wore" well and was useful in many ways. Mother hung unbleached muslin ruffles across The Pahlah windows. She handed me a soft, pliable, and lint-free unbleached muslin sack to dry the dishes. Some white muslin sacks had one decorated edge creating a border print. They made pretty pillowcases.

Haute couture or home *décor,* when we drove away from Southwest Flour and Feed we were assured of being feed-sack chic.

Chapter 28

MUSICALE

The culmination of a year's worth of piano lessons was a recital. Miss Emma Treadwell rented the Glendale Grammar School Auditorium, and all of her students, ranging in age from six-year-old Cricket to Natasha Cannova, the diva pianist, were seated in the side section of the hall. Only Mother was able to defer from participating in the recital because she was a grown-up. We were arranged loosely by age, but more specifically by talent and complexity of the songs we were to play.

The grammar school auditorium was a *grande dame* in the community. It was built in days before school performance halls became multipurpose rooms where lunches were served and basketball games played. Wooden aisles separated three distinct theater sections. Shabby padded seats folded up. Generations of school plays, choral concerts, band performances, and school board meetings had functioned on the creaky stage framed by faded velvet curtains.

By recital time I had progressed to "Spinning Song," a merry melody that I knew down to the last allegro. For the preceding months "doodle-doodle-dum-dum, dum-dum," wafted over The Ranch, the refrain permanently imbedded in my brain.

Cricket had prepared a half-minute rendition of "March of the Tin Soldiers." For two months he had been pounding out this two-line ditty. Miss Treadwell told him to play through it twice to add a bit of time to the routine. Cricket was the first musician on the program.

Mother and Daddy sat across the aisle from the waiting performers. Mother gripped the arms of her seat as her little maestro approached the stage. Cricket looked small and vulnerable. He wore a new white shirt for the occasion and blue short pants held up by over-the-shoulder button straps. His skinny legs ended in white socks and brown oxfords, old, but waxed to a soft gleam. Cleaned up, Cricket was kind of a cute kid.

Cricket glanced at Mother hesitantly, as if hoping to be rescued from the ordeal. Daddy winked at him, but I noticed he was hunched forward clutching tightly at his knees. Cricket squared his shoulders and marched up the stage steps in the tradition of the song he was about to perform. He bowed to the audience like a trained monkey then hopped up on the bench of the majestic Steinway.

An untamed cowlick fanned from Cricket's crown; it bobbed and waved as he pummeled the march. He ended the tune with a discordant flourish, leaped from the bench, and dashed for cover of the side curtains. The audience responded with a round of polite applause. The recital was underway.

Several junior prodigies performed after Cricket. Martha Metz curtsied demurely before exiting the stage after playing "Minuet." Bobby Grimes nodded curtly then scurried away after doing dastardly damage to "Volga Boatman." The audience applauded with relief as much as approval.

I awaited my turn on the sidelines. I, too, was scrubbed and scoured, and wedged into my Sunday best. I wore a crisp, blue organdy dress that Mother had made for Easter, a fashionable change from my usual chicken-linen school dresses. My heart pounded like a kettle drum. A miniature eraser had gone to work on my memory and eradicated everything I ever knew about "Spinning Song." The tune that I labored over for four previous months was suddenly a blank in my paralyzed mind. "How does it start! How does it start!"

"Dum-dum-dum-dum." NO!. "Diddle-dum. Diddle-dum" NO! "Dum-diddle, dum-dum." NO! Disassociated fragments of the song leapt maniacally through my head, but the refrain evaded my desperate recall. How could I escape this ordeal?

My muddled mind had not cleared when suddenly, my turn was upon me. I almost puked as I rose from my seat then sidled over three sets of knees between me and the end of the row. As I stepped into the aisle to begin my trembling ascent to the stage, my frilly dress caught on the arm of the last chair. I tugged impatiently, and it loosed from the grip of the chair, but not before a wide tear separated skirt from bodice. At this ungainly stage of my childhood, I seemed to have had a propensity for rending garments.

I whined. Then a glimmer of hope washed over me. Perhaps this was my respite. Perhaps I would not have to go through with this excruciating ordeal. The audience stirred restlessly wondering what accounted for the slight delay in the progression of musical numbers.

Miss Treadwell slipped her arm around my shoulder and bent over to whisper in my ear. "No one will notice…" "You'll be fine…" I recall her saying. This was my initiation to the tradition that the "show must go on." I marched down the aisle clutching disassociated parts of my dress with my left hand. Up the stage steps. I looked neither right nor left. My focus was on the grinning white teeth of the musical monster sitting center stage. I took my position on the bench, loosed my fingers from the dress, and placed them over the keys.

"Doodle-doodle-dum-dum." "Doodle-doodle-dum-dum." "Doodle-doodle-dum-dum." "Doodle-doodle-dum-dum." For an eternity I regaled the audience with repeated introductory measures of "Spinning Song," "doodle-doodle-dum-dum," "doodle-doodle-dum-dum," entreating my fingers to integrate the warps and wefts of the tapestry that formed the body of the song. On my nth attempt at the introductory bar of "Spinning Song" I completed the measure, "dum-dum," and I was off and spinning. I completed the air and fled the stage, not even remembering to hold my dress together.

Mother urged us to explore other outlets for our mediocre talents. Miss Zelda came to school every Tuesday afternoon and gave tap-dancing lessons to little girls. Actually, she encouraged boys to join the classes, but boys hung outside the windows and shouted rude interjections while a line of girls shuffled to the tune of "When April Showers Come Your Way." The entire semester of dance was in preparation for another recital.

Miss Zelda sent a costume pattern home, and Mother created plaid bloomers and an oilcloth raincoat that barely covered my rump. This and an umbrella was the costume for the April Showers part of the program. I would have preferred to wear the sequined cheesecloth of the Spring Fairies class.

Miss Zelda placed me inconspicuously at the end of the row. My plump legs pounded a beat behind my more lissome counterparts. Shuffle, shuffle, back, step. Heel, toe, step, step. We pranced and kicked ending with an extravagant flourish of twirling bumbershoots. Following the tap dance recital I put away my dancing shoes. I would have needed a bigger size next year, anyway.

When the school band teacher invited fourth graders to join the band, Mother took me to Quick's Music store in downtown Phoenix where Mr. Feldman whipped out a used clarinet, a cheap, metal learner's variety. He played a lively medley, his fingers dancing along the mysterious line of holes, levers, buttons, and pads lining the instrument. Twice a week I was excused from study period to meet with other beginners to squawk, bellow, and honk under the tutelage of Mr. Steffe. I reveled in every opportunity I could find to demonstrate my blossoming clarinet talent. On the playground. At the bus stop. On the bus. My friends held their ears and groaned when I opened my clarinet case.

At home I set up a music easel in The Pahlah. I screwed the black mouthpiece onto the stem of the clarinet, licked the reed, and clamped it in place. I took a deep breath and blew mightily. The resulting screech triggered a responding yowl from dog Betty, who sat outside under the window.

Clarinet: "Scritch! – Squawk! – Squall!" (Three – Blind – Mice).

Betty: "Yip! – Yap! – Yooow!"

Forever after, when I practiced my clarinet, I was accompanied note for note by Betty who yelped, yodeled, and yowled through the lesson.

Every grading period our general-music teacher made us sing solos for our grades. I am convinced that this experience cured me of ever aspiring to be a vocal musician. If a student got up in front of the class and warbled a song he was ensured of receiving an **A** in music on his report card. Otherwise, the grade would be lowered to a **C** or even a **D** if his decorum had not measured up. A lot of the boys refused to sing, elected to take the **C** in music, and be done with it. Most of the girls tried to find a melody they could execute. Josephine Jensen liked to perform. She always sang something that was on the top of the music charts. She was first to volunteer and self-assuredly chirruped an off-key interpretation of Dinah Shore's "Buttons and Bows."

I fretted about the assignment. I wasn't particularly taken with the selection of lyrics in our school music book, and I didn't know the words to popular songs being wailed over KTAR radio. I delayed my debut as long as I could, but when Music Teacher called my name I was suddenly on the spot. In that moment of sheer desperation I decided to sing a cowboy ballad that I picked up from Daddy. I occasionally heard him whistling and singing snippets of this mournful tune.

My legs were as limp as noodles as I made my way to the front of the class; my heart was in my gullet. I cleared my throat and belted out a lusty version of "When the Whorehouse Bells Are Ringing."

Music Teacher was stunned.

For the first time ever, I got a **D** in music.

Susan Harrison McMichael

When the Whorehouse Bells Are Ringing

Chapter 29
ZEKE THE GEEK

Most of the children that rode my bus to school boarded at farm labor camps. They were brown-skinned urchins who brought onto the bus the scars of living in poverty, miseries like ring-worm, lice, and scabies. I was one of the few pale-faces that made a thirty-mile round trip to and from school.

The bus lurched to a stop at Cluger's farm camp and the usual rag-tag collection of children embarked. I spread my books across the seat. I was saving the space for Sharon Watkins who would get on the bus when we reached her father's ranch house.

Cluger's had the motliest bunch of kids on the route. They were unwashed, uncombed, undisciplined. Rumor was that Cluger did not provide his camp with a functioning bathroom. Families carried their water from a communal spigot. Outhouses stood in a higgledy-piggledy row on the back perimeter of the camp site.

Those children were hot and smelly. Their clothes were soiled. As they jostled and pushed one another up the bus steps I averted my eyes and studied a point on the horizon. They shuffled around the bus and settled into empty seats.

The driver was ready to pull away from camp when a boy pounded on the closed door. I had never seen this kid. Some of the seasonal workers on the farms were "Okies." This boy must have been one of "them."

He stepped into the aisle timidly; his eyes searched for a place to sit. They landed on the empty seat that I had been saving.

"Kin I sit here?" he asked.

"This seat is saved," I informed him and returned to my study of the horizon. I secretly prayed that Sharon would not make me a liar by being absent that day.

He sighed and worked his way toward the back of the bus.

He was surly and had a gaunt scarecrow appearance. His outsized clothes hitched around him and gathered at his waist with a cord, his tennis shoes held together with adhesive tape.

That morning, after Teacher had posted attendance records at the door, the principal brought the new kid to my class and introduced him as Zeke. Zeke the Geek turned out to be the most dreadful boy in the room. He was in the White Birds' reading circle. Everyone knew the White Birds read first-grade books. His papers were a mess of scribbles, erasures, and holes. He missed almost all the words on his spelling tests. He hunkered at his desk and scowled at Teacher. He sidled to a corner table in the lunch room and waited idly while we opened our lunch boxes and shared contents.

Zeke's single coup was an Atom Bomb Ring. He called it the Lone Ranger Atom Bomb Ring, a curious moniker since the Lone Ranger was better known for silver bullets than for atom bombs. Coupons for this jewel were found on Kix cereal boxes. Zeke had wound tape through the loose ring to assure that the treasure did not fall off his finger. The tape became dirty and frayed. Zeke's finger turned green.

Zeke entertained a doltish circle of boys with this ring. He removed a red base from the cone-shaped trinket exposing a small lens. By peering into the lens, one saw tiny flashes of light that emulated the cataclysmic atom bomb blasts on Hiroshima and Nagasaki. The controversy of what this ring represented had not yet touched the elementary grades at Washington School.

Our class was gearing up for the annual Christmas Party. The room was festively decorated with red and green paper chains. Other bits of holiday art were pinned to the bulletin board. I was particularly proud of my construction paper Santa. His rotund body, his pointed hat, and a mittened right hand had been mimeographed on a piece of red construction paper. His face and a bag of toys were mimeographed on a piece of white construction paper. I had employed my full range of Crayolas to embellish a raggedy doll, a rocking horse, and a ball that peeped over the top of Santa's bulging bag. Then I guided my snub-nosed scissors around the outlined pattern. With lumps of library paste I adhered my artistic endeavors to the proper parts of Santa's anatomy. A piece of cotton completed the project, a parody of Santa's beard. Teacher added my masterpiece to a line of 27 elves waving right hands to the class.

Next to my Santa marched Zeke's Santa, by far the dopiest looking gnome on the bulletin board. Zeke had not colored his Santa decoration. Santa's expressionless face looked just as it emerged from the teacher's duplicating machine; the toys in Santa's pack remained dittoed ghosts. Santa's beard dangled from his left ear, and his right hand, minus a thumb, was raised in a defiant fist.

"We will draw names for our Christmas party gift exchange," Teacher announced at the end of the day. She produced a shoe box with 27 folded pieces of paper inside.

"The name that you draw from this box is to remain a secret. Before the Christmas party next Friday you should buy a 25-cent gift for the person whose name you pulled," Teacher continued.

I squirmed giddily as Teacher moved up and down the rows ensuring everyone pulled one folded paper from the box. "Oh, please, let me pick Martha, or even Helene," I silently implored.

With trepidation I unfolded my lot.

"Eek!" Of all the bad luck! Zeke was the name lettered on my paper. I couldn't believe that I would be expected to buy a Christmas present for Zeke the Geek!

A flurry of surreptitious switching of names began when students thought Teacher wasn't looking. But nobody that I asked wanted to trade names for Zeke. I rode the bus home in a blue huff and presented my unfortunate draw to Mother. Surely she would have a solution to my predicament.

"You can buy a toy for Zeke when we go to town again." Mother was matter-of-fact.

Mother took me to the Five and Dime on our next trip to town. Sprouse-Reitz packed on their shelves a medley of house wares and cleaning agents, yard goods and sewing notions, cosmetics and candy, tools and toys. I headed to the toy counter where I reluctantly combed the bins for a 25-cent contribution to the Christmas party. Glass strips on the counters segregated jump ropes from bubbles, jack sets from marbles, and yo-yos from rubber balls. I coveted a tiny tea set trimmed with delicate pink roses. I had enough money to buy Shirley Temple paper dolls or a Little Golden Book.

But, I had to spend my coin on a gift for Zeke the Geek! There were practical things like pencils and socks and combs. I was sure he could have used any of those items. I could purchase a little tin car, or a plastic cowboy on a rearing horse, or a bag of marbles, or a magic slate. I aimlessly picked up a magic slate and perversely sketched a goofy face, eyes crossed and tongue wagging. I obstinately wrote "Zeke the Geek" across the surface. When I lifted the gray shield covering the slate, the face mysteriously disappeared. Why couldn't Zeke disappear like the caricature on the slate?

However, next to the magic slates I found what I would buy for Zeke. I remembered Zeke's Santa, the Santa with a crooked beard, the Santa with the impassive face, the Santa whose toys were not colored, the Santa shaking his fist at the world. I would buy Zeke a box of Crayolas, eight sharp waxy crayons standing at attention in a yellow and green box. Papers wrapped tightly around slender rods of orange, red, violet, yellow, black, blue, brown, and green. They were not broken, peeled, or gnawed. I took the quarter from my pocket and smugly paid the clerk.

On the last day of school, before the much-anticipated Christmas vacation, I added a small parcel labeled "To Zeke from Susan" to the pile of gifts growing at the base of the classroom tree.

The Christmas party was the highlight of the school year. We cleared our desks of pencils and spelling tablets, of readers and composition books. Homeroom Mothers served cookies and punch. Tacks were removed from the construction paper Santas liberating them to appropriate artists. When Zeke's Santa was returned, he jammed it into his desk tearing Santa's arm in the process.

It was time to distribute the presents. I watched carefully as Teacher pulled gifts from under the tree and gave them to helpers who, in turn, delivered them to waiting students. Paper was ripped from the gifts and ribbon thrown into the aisles as classmates oohed and aahed over the toys they received. I watched Zeke out of the corner of my eye when he received my gift, then tore the colorful tissue covering the box of crayons. He immediately reached into his desk and pulled out his construction paper Santa. He began to color the toys in Santa's pack.

The children around me examined each other's presents. "What did you get?" they asked. My face flushed; tears pooled in my eyes. I buried my head in my arms on my desk. I had not gotten a present at the Christmas party.

But, wait. Teacher approached my desk. She held a wad of paper, lined primer paper, secured with layers of tape. It looked like a giant spit wad.

"Susan, this was behind the tree. We didn't see it until all of the other presents had been removed."

Scrawled in childish script, "To Susan."

I hesitantly received the small parcel. It looked like a depository for used bubble gum. I tore at the tightly folded paper. Eventually, I opened a ragged composition sheet.

The message in the center of this tattered primary writing paper said, "From Zeke." And, the Atom Bomb Ring, wound with dingy and frayed adhesive tape, fell on my desk.

*This chapter appeared in *Guidepost Magazine*, December 2003, in another form.

Chapter 30

HOW DOES YOUR GARDEN GROW?

In January our mailbox bulged with seed catalogs. Mother was transported to her roots. She poured over gorgeously illustrated pictures of Camellias, Azaleas, and Magnolias and envisioned a veritable antebellum garden enveloping Little House. She made copious lists that of flowers that surrounded her childhood home. Hydrangeas, shrubs that lined Alabama porches, spouting blue and lavender pom-poms as big as mop heads. Peonies, exploding in yellow, pink, white, rose, crimson, scarlet, and plum. Rhododendrons, spectacular hedges with fragrant funnel shaped flowers, blossoming in an array of colors along picket fences. Mother ached for the rich botanical tapestry of the South.

Seed companies did not discriminate geographically among the gardeners who received their catalogs. Nor were they absolutely forthcoming in their advice about the climate restrictions of the plants they hawked. The fact that we lived in the arid Southwest had little to no bearing on the flowers they promoted to us. If seeds were to be set in late spring by Eastern time-tables, they should have been planted in the Desert Southwest by the printing of the catalogs the November prior. Mother was pelted with pictures of homey garden flora – Aster, Rose of Sharon, Sweet William, Bleeding Heart, Spider Wort, Phlox. Mother ordered packages of seeds and dreamed of her landscape.

Wearily, Daddy listened to Mother's gardening plans. Tight-lipped, he axed through the hard-pan caliche then dug a trough across the front of the house. He dumped a wheel barrow full of chicken manure into the furrow and worked it into the "soil." Mother even convinced Daddy to scratch a handkerchief-sized patch beyond the flower bed. She would have a lawn.

Small envelopes of seeds arrived in a discreet brown package. Pictures on their packets were far more alluring than the tiny granules and pellets contained therein. Mother tenderly shook out a half-dozen measly specks from each packet and spooned them into her horticultural endeavor. She sprinkled precious water over the bed and waited for Eden to explode. In Arizona's warm March springtime the little seeds went to work and soon poked minuscule sprouts through the surface. But, by April, El Sol glared upon the interlopers; they gasped, wilted, and died.

We might not have had a garden worthy of feature in *Southern Living,* but around us, a wild and wanton explosion of spring color occurred. Desert-adapted wild flowers were hardy annuals, perennials, and shrubs that thrived on gravelly expanses of wasteland, along roadsides, on rocky slopes, and in dry gulches. Some of them tip-toed onto our property and settled in unlikely corners. Spots of desert color were scattered across the back field, around a rusty Ford chassis, behind the privy, and under fences. Odd tufts took root around rock and wood piles. They bloomed following winter rains.

Some flowers were delicate and shy, others robust and flamboyant. Fairy Dusters – light pink puffs with long stamens radiating from their centers. Desert Marigolds – eye-catching carpets of dense yellow. Mariposa Lilies – brilliant orange butterflies, reflecting their Spanish name. Globemallow, Sunflower, Arizona Poppy, Devil's Claw, Filaree – blossoms that thrived under the sun. Had Mother been able to tame them and incorporate them into a formal landscape, she would have had an exquisite garden, but these renegade plants were of a stubborn mind and could not be coaxed into the fertile trench in front of the house.

Cactus, too, wore crowns among their thorns. Stately Saguaros sprouted clusters of waxy white blossoms with yellow centers on the tips of their multiple arms. Other cactus plants resembled their namesakes – Beavertail, Hedgehog, Pin-Cushion, Barrel. They wore corsages of fuchsia, red, orange, and yellow. Even the devilish Cholla adorned its links with golden and bronze blooms.

About a dozen varieties of Prickly Pear crept along the desert floor. They were comprised of arrangements of flat pads laced with spines. They couldn't make up their minds about the jewelry they would don. Their flowers were yellow, red, or even purple among the same species.

One of the most peculiar specimens of the desert was the Century Plant. These curious plants, botanically known as the *agavi*, peppered dry, rocky slopes in regions north of us. One such plant had been transplanted to our land. It proceeded to send adventurous shoots from its base propagating a family of up-and-coming century plants in various stages of maturity. Grandmother Century Plant spent a long lifetime preparing to bloom, hence her name. When her moment of glory came, she looked like a giant asparagus sprouting out of an artichoke. Her base was a crown of fleshy gray-green spears tipped with mortal barbs. When the time was right (close to a century according to legend) a tall, thin stalk emerged from her heart. Within one month the stalk rose skyward 10-25 feet. We could actually see the stalk grow. Its daily progress could be measured in half-foot increments. Clusters of yellow flowers bloomed on the tips of horizontal branches near the top of the stalk. After pouring all of her energy into generating the massive shoot, Grandmother Century Plant's cycle was complete. She withered and died. Her progeny continued the procession of maturing until they, too, were ready to culminate their lives and send asparagus-like sprouts heavenward.

Most plants that weathered our climate were woody, thorny, or lethal. The Bougainvillea, though an import, was all three. Bougainvillea was discovered in Brazil in the mid 1700's. It gradually migrated to other warm climates around the globe where varieties spread dazzling arcs of color – pink, orange, and crimson. Here in the desert southwest Bougainvillea was a popular landscape choice both in town and in the country. Mother was captivated by wild bouquets that spilled over arbors and walls and radiated flaming color. She brought a small plant home from the nursery in town. Spindly and spiny, Bougainvillea took root, and then clambered up the front corner of Little House. Thorny branches with papery magenta blossoms encroached one side of the house then reached over the roof. Bougainvillea thrived under blistering sun and on little water. Nature had provided her with sap and barbs to discourage invasion from the outer world.

One day Mother pulled the rickety step ladder out of the garage. She armed herself with an array of clippers, snippers, and saws. She shrugged into one of Daddy's heavy khaki shirts and pulled a pair of canvas gloves over her wrists. She was setting out to trim the rambunctious branches of Bougainvillea.

From a precarious perch four feet off the ground, Mother reached toward the tangle of woody spines. The branches took on a life of their own, defying Mother to bring them into submission. As Mother reached toward one razor-laced stalk, another whipped around her. The branches grabbed at her hair, her collar, her skirt hem. They wrapped around her ankles, her arms, her neck. The fiery blossoms enveloping the side of the house seemed to chortle in devilish glee at the distress Bougainvillea inflicted.

Mother returned to the kitchen. Her shirt hung in ragged strips. She was riddled with scratches and contusions. Drops of blood seeped from angry welts on her arms. She looked as if she had gone to war with a wildcat.

The undisciplined Bougainvillea continued its diabolic ascent over the house.

Oh, for the gentle peaceful plants of Alabama! The South had its illusive majesty of the evening, a plant that showed its finery only after dark. The languid Moonflower Vine crawled over the ground, around fences, and up trellises. A white tubular flower opened at night and released powerful perfume guaranteeing allure to pollinating moths. With morning light, and with its singular purpose of attracting moths achieved, the

Moonflower's porcelain blossoms pinched shut. They withered and fell to the ground in limp shriveled masses.

In the desert we had the Night-Blooming Cereus. Most of the year, this cactus was decidedly unremarkable. Its bluish-grey twigs looked like dead sticks propped against the wall of our garage. One night in early summer – one night only – this Queen of the Night opened a single exquisite white bloom. In the fleeting evening hours a magnificent many-pointed white star unfolded, a star as big as a saucer, a star that outshone the lights of heaven. Its heavy sweet fragrance permeated the desert air. With the rays of the morning sun the blossom closed forever.

Chapter 31

TO BED WITH THE CHICKENS

"Goodnight, Mother. Goodnight, Daddy. Goodnight, Cricket." The scene mimicked bedtime in the suburbs.

Air-conditioning had not come to Arizona. The rich and the idle escaped to the mountains during July and August. The rest of us opened our windows, ran swamp coolers, and drank lots of water. We could endure a lot of heat in the daytime as long as we slept comfortably at night. In Phoenix, many homes had sleeping porches. These were screen-covered additions along one side of the house. Beds were lined along the porch, and the entire family slept there at night. A sleeping porch provided a bug-free (well, almost) environment and was a close alternative to sleeping under the stars. Some people hung a wet sheet at the end of the porch, and evening breezes blew through the fabric endowing the room with another layer of coolness.

Out at The Ranch, Little House squatted under the blistering July sun. Its corrugated iron roof captured the heat and dispersed it throughout our four square rooms creating an insufferable oven.

Morning chores were done. For lunch I nibbled on carrot sticks and hard boiled eggs; I sucked ice slivers that I had added to my tea. Sweat trickled down my neck, but I was engrossed in a Nancy Drew mystery. Mother sat next to the old Philco listening to the trials of *Stella Dallas*. She created a slight breeze with a cardboard fan that A.L. Moore and Sons

Mortuary distributed at last year's state fair. At 114°+ it was hard to find respite in the desert. Flies buzzed lethargically in the windows. Muslin curtains drooped indolently behind fly-speckled panes. The swamp cooler, mounted on a stand outside the parlor window, chugged and heaved. It merely rearranged the stultifying air.

Outside, Betty and Tige snoozed in hollows burrowed in the dusty shade of the tamarisks. Animals of the desert took refuge in their respective lairs. Another summer day in the desert.

El Sol arched over the firmament. His piercing glare reflected upon the parched land. Late in the day he reached the western horizon. He loosed his cloak and spread a magnificent mantel over the skyline – orange, magenta, purple, blue. Silhouetted against the royal colors were the mountains and cactus of the land. El Sol continued his descent and carried with him the heat of the day.

Now the critters of the desert ventured forth. Owls, bats, coyotes, tortoises, snakes. They knew better than to challenge El Sol in the daytime. Their primary business was conducted by moonlight.

We chose to be different. We worked during the day. At night, like the chickens, we went to bed. Through the night, heat from El Sol's afternoon scourge radiated throughout Little House. When we went to sleep, we wallowed and stewed in our own sweat.

Mother sought a solution. A take-off on the sleeping porch! The chicken coop nearest the house was not currently being used. It had been scrubbed and Lysoled after the last batch of pullets went to market. What better place to sleep? Like other chicken houses on The Ranch, this was an open-air construction, the bottom half wood lath, the upper half laced with chicken wire. It had a cement floor and a screen door.

To bed with the chickens. Mother and I set to work.

We dismantled the beds in the house. Off came the coverlets, and then the pillows, and then the sheets. Cricket and I slept on surplus army cots. We easily upended them and carried the canvas pallets across the yard. We pulled the lumpy mattress from the bed that Mother and Daddy shared and dragged it to the chicken coop. Off came the springs, the slats, the sideboards. At last only maple headboard and footboard remained to be transferred to our new sleeping quarters.

Then reconstruction began – same process in reverse. We set up headboard and footboard, pushed sides into their respective slots, spanned the sideboards with wooden slats, and set springs and mattress atop the whole affair. We placed the two army cots side by each. Clean sheets and clean coverlets, and we were ready for bedtime. Mother put a citrus crate next to her bed. She brought out a portable radio so she could listen to music before she fell asleep. She also set an alarm clock although that was a redundancy on a chicken farm. Roosters sounded reveille at a predictably early hour.

From then on summer nights were tolerable, even comfortable, for the desert cooled when the sun went down. The difference between daytime and nighttime temperatures varied as much as 30° during summer months.

Being sent to bed in the chicken house was not the same ordeal as being sent to bed in the real house. A moonlight drama played beyond the chicken-wire screen. The world around us came veritably alive. Stars winked at us, and occasionally a shooting star blazed through the firmament in a splendid display. A coyote yodeled, and his cohort responded from across the valley. An owl swooped from a nearby saguaro and seized a hapless field mouse as he ventured from his nest. A replay of our night in the tree house, only this time our beds were on terra firma, and we were ensconced behind board walls and screens.

We listened to our neighbors, the hens next door, as they fluffed and bustled about getting ready for bed. They clucked and cooed then settled on their roosts for the night. Cricket and I pulled our sheets to our chins and fell asleep, too.

One night the entire family was abed in the chicken house. Cricket and I had gone out at our earlier bedtime. Mother and Daddy came out sometime later. For a while they listened to the radio then they fell asleep as the radio softly played. All was serene.

A nocturnal creature made his way over the land. He was looking for anything that might satisfy his hunger – beetles, grubs, grasshoppers, lizards, rodents, eggs, fruit. He was not discriminating. He snuffled around; he dug under rocks and debris. He made his way into the side yard of the chicken house where we slept. There were no chickens, but he explored further.

The sleeping house, like all of our chicken houses, had a trap door that let into a side yard. When chickens were in residence, an open door allowed them to move freely between the yard and the house. The trap door in our sleeping house was loose. The midnight marauder stuck his nose through the opening and discovered he could slip through.

Once inside, he fluffed his fur, shook his black and white striped tail, and meandered up and down the aisles between our beds. His scratching paws roused us from our slumber. We lay in paralyzed anticipation. Finally, not having found a morsel to assuage his hunger, he slowly made his way back to the trap door and slipped into the night.

Daddy nailed the trap door shut the next morning.

Chapter 32

WE'LL KILL THE OLD RED ROOSTER WHEN THEY COME

"A chicken farm!"
"Can you imagine!"
"They even have an out-house!"
Our relatives lived in civilized places. From their porches swings in the gentle South they speculated about our crude existence.

They were bemused and somewhat embarrassed to be related to us renegades. Kindly folk, they were accustomed to household help, garden clubs, and swee'tea in the afternoon. But, on occasion, an adventurous segment of the family headed west to see how the other side lived. When we expected company we pulled out all the stops.

Mother tackled the house to get it "readied up." She hung Navajo rugs over the fence and knocked dust from their fibers with a carpet beater. She scrubbed cement floors, wiped fingerprints from the door jambs, scoured kitchen cabinets, and alphabetized spice boxes. She lined books neatly on their citrus-crate shelves, removed feed-sack curtains from the windows, ran them through Water Witch, starched them like stiff pennants, and washed fly specks off the window panes. She gathered orphan Monopoly pieces and Domino tiles and tucked them into catch-all baskets along with pencil stubs, thumb tacks, corks, nut picks, and miscellaneous keys to unknown locks. She whisked away Daddy's poultry journals and his highway plans and stacked them in the garage.

Outside, Cricket and I were put to work raking the grounds. Mother wanted the area outside the kitchen door (which was the entrance to the house) to be raked so that tine marks in the gravel marched in a uniform north/south direction. Cricket and I chased one another dragging our garden rakes to accomplish the landscape pattern Mother desired. Mother planted a few nursery-grown marigolds under the front window and set potted geraniums on either side of the door.

We set up a proper bed again in the bedroom and lined extra cots in the chicken house aka sleeping quarters. As long as our guests did not expect the amenities of the Waldorf Astoria, we could accommodate the army of a small principality.

Aunt Mamie came to see us. Prim, proper Mamie Johnston (with a "T") Sims from Texarkana. We met the Southern Pacific at Phoenix Union Station and carted Aunt Mamie to The Ranch. Aunt Mamie dressed in black and smelled like lilacs. She had blue hair contoured into rigid waves against her head. She wore corsets and stockings and old-lady shoes.

"My, my. Isn't this rustic?" Aunt Mamie surveyed our accoutrements.

Aunt Mamie was as out of place on our ranch as a Duchess at a dog fight. She heeded Mother's caution to shake her footwear before she dressed in the morning. And, early each day we heard a vigorous pounding. Thump. Thump. Thump. Then again. Thump. Thump. Thump. Aunt Mamie was beating her sensible shoes firmly against the bedposts. She emerged at breakfast, fully composed, attired in black crepe, corseted, stockinged, her lace-up shoes assuredly rid of any scorpions that had possibly crawled in during the night.

Aunt Mamie attempted to teach us some finer points of Southern living.

"Elsie, Deah," she offered, "I want to share this mahvelous aspic recipe that Nicey makes for the Maydale Society when it is my turn to entertain." Nicey was Aunt Mamie's housekeeper. Tomato Jelly was a peculiar taste to our palates. We cautiously pushed uneaten portions under our lettuce leafs.

According to Aunt Mamie, a fine young lady never let her hands be idle. Come late afternoon, she routed me from the mire of the ranch yard and supplied me with a crochet hook and a ball of twine. With hopeless resolve, she set about teaching me the art of crochet. The resultant knot-riddled doily was a gnarl of slipped stitches and tangled chains.

One amusement that Aunt Mamie introduced to The Ranch caught our fancy. Canasta was a popular game circulating among afternoon card parties in the South. We whiled away hot afternoons in cunning three-handed competition.

"Didn't you study engineering in college, William?" Aunt Mamie watched her star nephew while he mucked out a chicken pen.

One Sunday morning Aunt Mamie rustled to the breakfast table wearing a fine black georgette dressmaker suit with a matching peplum jacket. Two long strands of jet beads clicked about her neck. She looked like the Queen Mother. After breakfast, she pinned a black straw hat over her blue coif, and pulled black suede gloves over her fingers. Aunt Mamie had decided to amend our errant church-going ways.

Mother and Daddy were both from dour Presbyterian backgrounds. We maintained a membership and a quasi attendance record among the frozen-chosen at First Presbyterian Church in downtown Phoenix. Crisis after crisis, project after project on The Ranch kept us terra firma bound most Sundays. The distance into Phoenix was great, and attending church held modest priority.

"Elsie and I have to bow out," said Daddy. "But, the children can go with you."

Mother hustled Cricket and me into Sunday School attire. Daddy gave each of us a dime to drop into the offering plate.

Daddy handed Aunt Mamie the keys to the pickup truck along with a map that he had sketched on the back of an envelope. "Watch the brakes. Pump them two or three times and allow plenty of room to stop."

Aunt Mamie perched on the edge of the pickup seat. Her toes barely touched the pedals. She gripped the steering wheel and peered anxiously over its rim. We lurched and bolted out the gate. Gradually, Aunt Mamie brought the speedometer up to a quivering 25 miles-per-hour. Making no allowance for dips, ruts, jackrabbits, or farm wagons, we navigated ranch country at a trembling pace. We bounced along dirt roads, past alfalfa fields, by farm labor camps. As we approached the outskirts of Phoenix traffic increased. By then we were driving on pavement, but 25 miles-per-hour was Aunt Mamie's concept of universal velocity. She continued through the metropolis undeterred by cars that honked and whipped around us.

"There it is," I squealed as we eventually came in sight of the church belfry. The church was located on busy Monroe Street. "Cricket and I go to our classes on this side."

"You children jump out. I will find a place to park." Aunt Mamie pulled up to the Sunday School entrance. "I will meet you after church."

Gripping our "Jesus and the Little Children" color pages, Cricket and I set about to find Aunt Mamie after Sunday School. She was sipping coffee in the church patio, visiting with society ladies of Phoenix who hovered over lace-covered tables and silver-plated servers during the social fête after church. We said our good-byes and headed for the parked pickup. Aunt Mamie led us purposefully in an easterly direction for half a block. Then her stride slowed. At the first corner we turned south. At another corner we walked west. And, at still another corner, we turned south again, and again west. We had circumnavigated A.L. Moore and Sons Mortuary and found ourselves on busy 7th Avenue. We could still see the spires of the church, but we were two blocks away as the crow flies.

We made our way back to the church and set out in another direction. Across the street from the church and on the back side was a seedy used car lot, "Honest Abe's." Maybe Abe was playing upon his proximity to the church for his image. Red, blue, and green pennants fluttered from cables surrounding the lot. Honest Abe was one of the few enterprises in Phoenix open for business on a Sunday. Several people milled around the lot kicking tires and looking under hoods. Our dusty pickup was nestled right where Aunt Mamie had parked it, between an aging Buick Roadmaster and a Packard sedan, both heralding low, low prices splashed across their windows in white tempera. Abe watched us, hands on hips, as Aunt Mamie see-sawed back and forth extricating the dusty pickup from its tight parking confines. Fortunately, Abe had not sold our vehicle while we were in church. Unfortunately, the Packard sedan spouted one more dent in its back fender before we got out.

Alabama cousins came. Aunt Gladys and Uncle John accompanied by two pugnacious little boys, Johnny and Turner. They teamed up with my kid brother and proceeded to make my life miserable. That I persisted in consorting with them is an indication of my starvation for playmates. In one playtime scenario we set up camp as a tribe of wild Indians. I was appointed to be the sacrificial "squaw." They tied me to a fence post and built a pyre at its base. Our festering resentments toward each other came to a head one day when I climbed up onto our tree-house platform with a bucketful of dry horse apples and began pelting the boys as they tried to climb the ladder. They, in turn, fortified themselves with a bucket of not-so-dry grenades of the same origin and hurled them upwards at me. The shaggy tamarisk branches deflected most of the missiles. To my delight the fecund bombs rained back on the boys. Aunt Gladys was at her wits end trying valiantly to keep her boys' knickers clean and pressed on our gritty spread.

Aunt Gladys was a school teacher in Montgomery. In college she had studied Spanish. She accompanied Mother and me to McElroy's where we purchased fresh milk. José, McElroy's handyman, got the milk for us from a walk-in cooler. José's English was halting; we communicated with him through sign language and smiles. Aunt Gladys decided to put her rusty Spanish to use. She explained to José that that Mother was her sister. Her Spanish vocabulary was not strong enough to inform José that Mother was actually her sister-in-law.

"Hermosa." She pointed to Mother

José grinned and nodded.

"Hermosa." Aunt Gladys smugly repeated.

José acknowledged his apparent understanding of her

message by continuing to grin and nod.

"*Hermosa.*"

Mother put the jug of milk on the floor of the pickup, and we returned to The Ranch.

"My gosh, Elsie!" Aunt Gladys yelped after we got back. "I believe I told that Mexican that you were beautiful. How embarrassing! *Hermana!* That's the Spanish word for sister!"

When we occasioned to have company we tried to introduce them to the wonders of Arizona. We might make a journey to the Grand Canyon or to the Painted Desert and Petrified Forest. We made one such trip with Grandmama Seale, Aunt Nell, Aunt Peggy, Uncle Jay, and sullen cousin Ron. On this particular trip we drove two-car tandem, the more sedate of the grownups riding in our company's upscale automobile, the rest of us piling in the ranch pickup. Kids elected to ride in the back end of the pickup; Mother drove. Up in canyon country we stopped at a scenic point for a picnic. As Mother turned the truck around near the edge of a ravine, the back tires edged perilously close to the gorge. Six wide eyes peered over the tailgate into the yawning abyss. In one terrifying moment, a rear tire dropped over the edge of the chasm. The remaining rear tire spun wildly to secure purchase in the sand. The truck bolted forward, then shimmied to safety in a quivering stop parallel to the sheer drop.

When Mother realized how close she had come to going into the ravine she scolded me. "Susan, why on earth didn't you let me know I was so close to the edge!" Was this tacit permission to call Mother to task when she might be in error?

On the long drive home from the Grand Canyon we proceeded over the same bumpy road our family had taken when we moved to The Ranch – the Black Canyon Stage Route. We were in need of a comfort station. Grandmama Seale, Aunt Nell, and Aunt Peggy were a step above using nature's facilities.

Mayer was a mining/ranching community. A few dilapidated homes, dark and shuttered for the night, dotted the trail as we approached a wide spot in the road. A gas station, a bar, and a general store indicated that we were in metropolitan

Mayer. Only one of these establishments was open so late in the evening. We piled out of car and pickup and streamed in. A man stood behind a long bar polishing glasses. A couple of cowboys slouched at the counter. A card game was going on in another corner of the room. Grizzled ranchers clinching cigarettes between their teeth stoically studied their splayed cards. A juke box blared in the background – Kitty Wells wailing, "It Wasn't God Who Made Honky Tonk Angels."

Our spectacular entrance prompted immediate silence in the room. The medley ground to a morose finale – ". . .that has caused many a good girl to go wrong."

The card game stopped mid-wager.

Aunt Peggy stepped forward and made the request.

"Excuse me. Wheah is the powdah room?"

The bartender jerked his thumb toward an open door at the rear of the room. We paraded that direction. The door led outside, down some rickety steps, and along a weed-studded lane. We fumbled the length of the dark path and ended up at a wooden stall replete with a crescent moon on the door.

Wheah Is the Powdah Room?

Most people who came to see us never came back. I reckon they were glad to leave after a week of rationed water, hard cots, and blistering sun.

Chapter 33
SHE'S FLOWN THE COOP

... special news bulletin. Phoenix Police are searching... KTAR morning news cackled the alarming report that Winnie Ruth Judd had escaped ... again. Mother turned the dial so that she could better hear the grim details.
Winnie Ruth Judd. Her very name sent shivers down the spine. On the playground we jumped rope to the chant:

> *Oh Winnie Ruth took an ax*
> *And gave her girl friend forty whacks.*
> *When she saw what she had done*
> *She gave another forty-one.*
>
> *H! – Hot pepper (rope beats fast)*
> *E! – Elevator (rope goes up)*
> *L! – Limbo (rope goes down)*
> *P! – Popcorn (rope wiggles)*
>
> *Dum dum do do*
> *Catch me if you can*
> *I can jump faster*
> *Than Winnie Ruth can*

And now Winnie Ruth was loose again, probably with her ax and her trunk. Not since Lizzie Borden did a woman's name strike such terror.

Mother snapped the radio off. She tied the strings of her floppy straw hat under her chin. It was time to check the new brood of baby chicks. She told us to stay near the house today.

The sun cocked an eye over the horizon. Chanticleer lustily announced the dawn. What would this day bring? Life began to stir around The Ranch. Little red hens waddled off of their nests in search of bugs and grain. Turkeys drifted from their perch in the tamarisks. Dogs thumped their tails on the packed earth outside the kitchen door.

New baby chicks huddled in a downy morning mass under the brooder lamp. Mother checked the spigots to make sure water dripped fresh and clean. She added mash to the feed troughs. She assured herself that none of the weaker babes had died during the night as a result of suffocation, or even worse, as a result of wicked siblings pecking him to death. Mother returned to the kitchen and clicked the radio back on.

"Phoenix Police and personnel at the Arizona State Hospital are seeking information concerning the whereabouts of legendary trunk murderess, Winnie Ruth Judd. Believed to still be in the vicinity..."

Mother continued her rounds of the chicken coops. She opened the shutters to the side pens. Chickens flocked to the outer yards. Mother checked their water. She filled food troughs with prescribed grain. She collected eggs in the hen house. She returned to the kitchen and clicked the radio back on.

"Police are still searching..."

Mother flipped the lever of the pump that would bring water to the house for the remainder of the day. She pulled hoses to the laundry shed and filled Water Witch. For the rest of the morning she spun clothes through its churning bowels and into two awaiting galvanized rinse tubs. Billowing sheets and faded dungarees danced along the clothesline.

"Any information leading to the capture of..."

Sixteen years had passed since the grisly episode, but Phoenix and all of Arizona still resonated from the gruesome trunk murders purported to have been committed by Winnie Ruth Judd. Her very name struck terror among local children.

Mothers at the ends of their ropes with childish misbehavior, threatened ominously to turn miscreants to the fearsome clutches of Winnie Ruth Judd.

The legend that hovered around Winnie Ruth dated back to 1931. Winnie Ruth, allegedly, hacked to death her two best friends, stuffed their dismembered bodies in trunks and shipped them via Union Pacific to Los Angeles.

The real story was far more complicated and not really understood. Winnie Ruth was a pretty, young medical secretary married to a doctor who had moved to Los Angeles looking for work in a medical clinic. In his absence, Winnie and her two friends moved among a scandalous social set. Criminal overtones included illegal booze and prostitution. An unacceptable love affair and jealousy were thrown into the mix. The grisly deed followed an argument at a seamy party. The two women friends were shot to death before they were dissected. Purportedly, Winnie stuffed their fragmented bodies into the luggage and bought tickets for herself and the trunks to California.

The macabre deed was discovered by a baggage handler who was overcome by a nauseous odor permeating the luggage and an oozing substance that turned out to be blood. Pretty Winnie Ruth was escorted back to Phoenix where she was tried for murder. She was found guilty and sentenced to death by hanging. She was moved to the state prison to await execution. Just 72 hours before the scheduled execution, Winnie Ruth was pronounced criminally insane and committed to the Arizona State Hospital where she remained as a prisoner/patient. But, she proved adroit in the art of escape.

"Winnie Ruth Judd wandered off the hospital grounds ... has been missing..."

Mother drained the laundry tubs. She pegged the last load of denims on the line. She called us in to lunch and opened a can of vegetable soup.

Afternoon chores: Mother got out the Singer and stitched knee patches on Little Cricket's Wranglers. She hemmed new dish towels made out of bleached feed sacks. She washed and sorted beans and cautiously put them in the pressure cooker to rattle and dance. Then she sat for a while to read a story in the *Saturday Evening Post*.

Near supper time: The sun tilted on the western horizon. Mother checked the beans adding chili and an extra dose of cumin. She stood at the stove stirring the cauldron. The kitchen door rattled. We were startled because visitors to The Ranch were few and far between.

Mother gasped. Cricket and I hovered around her skirt. From the window we saw a dented pickup parked inside the gate. Someone rapped urgently at the door. Through the screen we saw a mountainous figure draped in multiple layers of denim and calico. It wore a fringed leather vest, boots, and thick stockings rolled over the tops. Hair, pulled into a severe bun, was coming loose. Grey tendrils formed a spiked halo.

"*Notify the Phoenix Police if you have evidence of the whereabouts of ...*"

Mother garnered her courage. She pushed Cricket and me toward The Pahlah. She grabbed a butcher knife and edged to the door.

"I'm sorry to bother you ma'am," the apparition began. "I am looking for Blanding's Place."

"Blanding's Place?" Mother stuttered.

"Yes, Ike Blanding. He sold me a nanny goat. I'm supposed to pick it up today, but I can't find his place."

"Blanding's Place," Mother repeated. Then she came to her senses. She probably would not have to employ the butcher knife.

"Ike Blanding lives another mile down the road. There is a water tower where the road forks. His gate is just beyond the water tower."

"Thank you, ma'am," our intruder chortled. "Have a good evenin'."

Mother dropped the butcher knife and sank into the rocking chair. The beans bubbled and plopped.

"*Phoenix Police apprehended Winnie Ruth Judd twelve hours after she was discovered missing. She was returned to Arizona State Hospital.*"

Chapter 34

EGG-SPERIMENT

"How to Make a Raft." Daddy's *Boy Scout Yearbook* (circa 1916) went on to say that a Scout's necessity for a raft usually occurred in cross-country traveling when he possessed no other tools than a hatchet and a knife.

I discarded the notion of building a floatation device. The simplicity of the tools needed to build a raft was offset by the need for logs and poles and lashings woefully lacking on The Ranch. Besides, streams that periodically meandered along irrigation ditches were shallow and easily jumped. No raft needed.

The handbook was full of stories and endurance tips generally useful for survival in a wilderness. Some of the outdoor tips I put on hold thinking they'd be worth trying sometime. "How to Make a Fire Without Matches." That would be a mighty good stunt. (However, what kind of Scout went into the wilderness without matches?) "How to Tie a Tourniquet Knot." I could try this restraint on Cricket. (Handy, perhaps, if a buddy Scout were maimed wielding a hatchet as he constructed a raft.)

But, "How to Keep Eggs Fresh in Camp" had an immediate and practical application. Our limited ice-box space created a frequent dilemma when we needed to keep food items chilled. Here was a way for Mother to keep her eggs fresh.

According to the Boy Scout Yearbook, a skillful scout

found a cool shady spot and dug a hole about six inches deep. I wasn't going to find a cool spot, but I'd look for a hidey-hole in the shadows. Then Skillful Scout lined the hole with a thick layer of excelsior. I had that material at my fingertips. Daddy had just changed our cooler pad. The discarded excelsior had not yet gone to the incinerator. Skillful Scout placed eggs in the bed of excelsior and then covered them with another thick layer. Lastly, Skillful Scout put stakes around the hole to keep people from walking into it.

I planned to create a subterranean egg shelter. I selected a site behind the hen house. This was the very location where Betty had birthed her litter of puppies when we first moved to The Ranch. The scrubby mesquite that had once sheltered a new mom and her whimpering family now cast dusty shadows on hard-packed earth. I figured this would be a good location for my earthen "ice-box."

I rummaged among the tools in the garage and pulled out a shovel and a hoe. Excavation of a small hole in the ground turned out to be easier said than done. I chopped at the desired site with the hoe to break the inhospitable caliche. Caliche is a layer of soil in which earthen particles have been cemented together by lime deposits. Digging into caliche is like digging into a sidewalk. The hoe bounced, and the dirt skittered. Plink, plink. Nicks and scratches were all I had to show for my endeavor.

Then, I thought to soften the ground by sprinkling it with water. I took off in search of a hose. The nearest hose was siphoning water from the well to the orange trees. I interrupted its watering cycle. I loosed the hose from its tap at the well, dragged it across the ranch yard, and attached it to a water faucet located beside the hen house. I turned water onto the parched ground. Moisture did not immediately soften the hardpan. I left the hose to trickle on the proposed site of my quarry. When I returned to my project, water had spread extravagantly. Mother would scold if she saw such a careless waste of water. I hoped the summer sun would dry up evidence of my indiscretion.

Digging was easier after the ground was soaked. Between

the hoe – plink, plink – and the shovel – scritch, scratch – I eked out a hole the requisite six inches deep for my egg-burial. I retrieved a bundle of moldy excelsior from the discarded cooler pad and lined my hole with straw-like material. I now needed eggs to complete my project.

At the tender age of eight I suffered from a hint of alektorophobia; I was scared of the hens. Hens were bossy peevish creatures that squabbled among themselves. They were possessive of their products and assailed me when I attempted to extract eggs from beneath their ruffles.

"Don't let the hens know you are afraid," Mother admonished.

And day after day, Mother handed me a basket and sent me to the hen house to surmount my fear.

Before cracking the hen house door, I stopped to wipe my clammy hands on the sides of my jeans.

"Aaaw!" I kicked the door to shoo any biddies from the opening and to prevent their escape into the larger ranch yard.

As I sidled in, I immediately sensed an element of conspiracy among the tenants. Hens bustled inside the coop. They drew together in a circle where they clacked and clattered messages in code. The hairs on the back of my neck tingled.

A few hens scratched for bugs in the side yard, but they kept a wary eye cocked toward the disruption in the hen house. My heart jumped to my throat.

I most dreaded the nesting hens, for they were insolent and domineering. And, there were always two or three hens who sat defiantly on their nests protecting their progeny. Beads of sweat lined my brow.

First I recovered eggs from the boxes lined along the wall that were not being guarded. Then I checked the floor. Sometimes a hen settled herself in a corner of the coop and deposited her offering on the hard cement. Finally, I tackled those boxes occupied by redoubtable hens.

Sure enough, Attila the Hen was guarding her nest at the time. She gave me a one-eyed glare. Since fowl have eyes on the sides of their heads I saw only one beady eye.

I coaxed, "Nice Henny, do you have an egg for me

today?" I reached timidly toward her ruffles.

Attila clucked. I jumped back egg-less.

I begged, "Please don't peck me." I reached again.

She squawked and flapped her wings. I retreated egg-less again.

I threatened, "Give me your egg, or we'll throw you in a stew pot."

At that she rose to the bait. She screeched and flew in my face before landing indignantly on the floor. The rest of the harem encircled her in feathery resentment, and they resumed their agitated chatter.

This scene repeated every time I entered the hen house. Sometimes I retrieved the protected egg unscathed. Sometimes I dropped it. Sometimes I crushed it in my hand.

Each day for a week I appropriated one or two eggs before I returned the collection to the kitchen. I carefully placed the pilfered eggs in my hole and swathed each deposit with excelsior insulation. I further covered the hole with a board and a rock to discourage dogs or vermin from finding the eggs. Mother seemed not to notice a shortage in our egg intake. A dozen or so eggs incubated in a subterranean vault for the remainder of the summer. In the meantime I forgot about my project.

Fall was upon us. School was well underway before my memory was jogged about my egg-speriment. One Saturday I unearthed the eggs and presented them for Mother's approval.

"How long have they been in the ground?"

"Not so long," I mumbled. "They should still be fresh."

Mother did not even crack an egg from my purloined cache. She relegated the suspect dozen to the incinerator. When garbage was next burned the odor that lingered was that of a bad breakfast.

Chapter 35
GOLDEN COCKS

Easter Bunny left two deliveries at the kitchen door. The baskets were filled with jellybeans, marshmallow pips, and chocolate bunnies. Each basket also contained a suspiciously familiar box aerated by small holes.

In my box a black puff with beady chicklet eyes cheeped unhappily. In Cricket's box a yellow puff blinked. Not until I examined my new pet did I realize that chicken eyelids opened from the bottom up.

"Golly, gee!" I exclaimed and added this bit of trivia to my on-going education on chickens.

The little chicks' lower fringe-laced eyelids winked eerily upward giving them a slightly askew countenance. These were bantam chicks, midget versions of the chickens Mother and Daddy raised for market.

Pip and Squeak were understandably stressed. They came to us via Glendale Hatchery along with a regular order of chicks that Mother picked up earlier in the week. Mother had helped Easter Bunny by nurturing the bantams for several days without our knowing it.

We nestled the bantams in a small cage beside the kitchen stove. They were greedy little buggers. They quarreled and cheeped and tussled over morsels in their enclosure. According to Jiggs at the hatchery, bantam chickens enjoyed attention and handling more than large breeds. They would progress through the same stages as their larger counterparts, but in maturity they would be only one-fourth or one-fifth the weight of standard poultry breeds.

We kept Pip and Squeak beside the stove until feathers replaced soft down; then we moved them to a larger cage in the barn. They became accustomed to the coddling that Cricket and I administered. They expected handfuls of choice corn.

As they developed it was evident we had two cockerels on our hands. Pip and Squeak seemed like silly names.

"You could rename them," Mother suggested. "There is a famous rooster from literature named Chanticleer."

"And," she continued, "What about Napoleon? Napoleon was a famous general. He was a small man with a big ego."

Pip and Squeak became Chanticleer and Napoleon.

Time came when we turned the bantams loose on the ranch. In the mornings we let them out of their cages, and they were free to scratch about the land for bugs and grubs and seeds. In the evenings we lured them back to their cages with plates of grain.

Chanticleer was a rose-comb bantam, an iridescent black bird. His plumage shimmered between black and deep shades of purple, pink, green, and blue as he strutted and preened about his fiefdom. His topknot was a fleshy gnarled protuberance that did, indeed, look like an open rose.

Napoleon was golden. His magnificent tail was a fan of green and blue plumes. His single serrated comb waved cockily atop his head.

Chanticleer and Napoleon were positive martinets. They seemed to know that their lot was different from that of the masses in the chicken coops. They swaggered about The Ranch as the multitudes gibbered and pecked behind wire mesh confines.

Arizona State Fair was about to open. Colorful posters nailed to fence posts along the road invited entries. Horses and cows and pigs. Oh, my! Rabbits and sheep and goats. Oh, my! Ducks and geese and chickens. Oh, my!

"Let's enter Chanticleer and Napoleon in the fair!" I was

sure that our magnificent fowl would capture top honors in the poultry division.

I wrote to the fair officials and requested entrance forms. Mother helped us complete the applications. We submitted them along with the modest fees.

The day before the fair opened exhibiters were setting up displays. Livestock species were unloaded in their respective barns. Cricket and I cradled wire cages while we waited in line at the poultry building. A grumpy man at the registration table viewed our entries.

"Them ain't show fowl," he barked. "There's no point entering them at this fair." He dismissed us abruptly and proceeded to check in the next person in line.

Crestfallen, Cricket and I carried our rejected roosters back to the pickup and back to The Ranch.

Later in the week we returned to the State Fair as visitors. Mother took us through each exhibition building. We looked at every horse, every cow, every pig, every rabbit, every sheep, every goat. And when we got to the poultry building, we systematically worked our way along row upon row of cages.

There was a stunning variety among the birds. Black Minorcas, White Plymouth Rocks, Buff Orphingtons, Rhode Island Reds, and, these were just the regular chickens. There were Araucanas, Blue Andalusians, Mottled Houdans, and Silver Laced Wyandottes. These fowl seemed to know they were the cream of the flock.

But, in my humble opinion, Chanticleer and Napoleon were as regal as any cock on display. In the middle of a long row two empty cages, side by side, bore entry labels. "Chanticleer, Bantam Rooster, owner, Susan Harrison". "Napoleon, Bantam Rooster, owner, Cricket Harrison."

Following their rejection at the Arizona State Fair, Chanticleer and Napoleon acted like disgruntled hooligans. They resorted to insolent tyranny; as a pair they struck alarm in the farmyard, at least for one little girl. My reaction to their increasingly audacious behavior mounted to sheer terror. Perhaps it was because one raked me with his spur as I put him back in his cage one evening. I, in turn, slammed the rooster against the wires. The line was drawn, and we were at war.

The feisty cocks took to chasing me relentlessly around the ranch. If I opened the kitchen door, they strutted forth daring me to step outside. If I played hop-scotch on the packed earth, they flapped madly at me dusting my stick-drawn squares in their wake. If I bounced a ball off the side of the garage, they materialized aggressively. I hurled the ball at them and took off like a banshee. Two miniature cocks screeched at my heels.

"They only chase you because you run." Mother was unsympathetic.

For an entire season I took my outdoor activities in small doses, punctuated by frantic races across the yard.

Days were getting longer again. The bantams now roosted in the orange trees. At the crack of dawn they performed their ritual reveille. The Ranch came to life.

One spring morning Mother found a trail of black feathers scattered through the orange grove. The plumes were no longer shiny and iridescent. Rather, they were dusty and bent. We surmised that a hungry coyote had come onto the property in search of dinner. He tangled with a midget rooster. The coyote apparently got the upper hand but not without a fight.

Napoleon continued to scratch and peck about the ranch yard for bugs and grubs. He didn't wander far from the barn. At sunrise he crowed listlessly, more like he had a lump in his throat. And he never again chased a little girl around The Ranch.

Chapter 36
NOBODY HOME BUT US CHICKENS

Mother and Daddy's social calendar was woefully blank. Mother's interpretation of a social event was a PTA meeting at Washington School. Then she donned a freshly starched chicken-linen dress, clasped a turquoise-studded squash-blossom (a stunning Navajo necklace) around her neck, and bustled to the affair.

Generally, Mother was occupied with daily survival on the ranch, the routine of placating irascible fowl, of leeching water from the inconsistent well, of keeping body and soul together. Nurturer, healer, teacher, cook, seamstress, laundress, coordinator of respectability.

Daddy spent the week on highway construction jobs. He was not interested in further social life. He rattled in on Friday night and assumed the role of weekend chicken wrangler. He sterilized coops for new batches of chicks and tinkered with the well. He poured over poultry catalogs to glean information about new techniques for gainful farming and agonized over ledgers that showed marginal profits. He fell asleep reading *Riders of the Purple Sage* (Zane Grey) or *Through the Grand Canyon from Wyoming to Mexico* (Ellsworth Kolb). Engineer, farmer, handyman, carpenter, mechanic, businessman, Western scholar.

I figured that their lives were complete. They had the ranch, and they had Cricket and me. The ranch extracted human servitude, as I suppose, two children extracted emotional energies. Of course, there were regular errands, occasional appointments, and shopping excursions related to the ranch or to us children. There were no baby sitters. Mother and Daddy bundled up Cricket and me and carted us along.

One summer morning the tables turned. Mother and Daddy had a business appointment, and they did not want to take Cricket and me. I caught murmured bits of their conversation.

"Nine o'clock."
"Mr. Moeller."
"Valley National Bank."

This was obviously a meeting of some importance. Mother opened a new package of nylon stockings. She drew them over her toes, guided them expertly up her legs, and checked to see that the seams were straight in back before snapping them onto tabs that dangled from her girdle. Mother slipped into a grey linen shirtwaist dress and clipped a brooch on her collar.

Daddy shined his shoes, donned a fresh pair of starched khakis, knotted a tie at the throat of his white shirt, and plopped his dress-up fedora atop his head.

The day was bright and clear. Mother and Daddy expected to be back by the noon hour.

"We are going to leave you at home," said Mother.

Daddy sweetened the deal for me. "We will pay you fifty cents to take care of Cricket and watch the house."

At nine years old this was my first paying job. I embraced it with zeal. Cricket and I stood at the gate and waved as Mother and Daddy rolled away. I conscientiously assumed my role as Ruler of the Roost.

"Cricket, let's play *Old Maid.*" We had a partial deck of kiddie playing cards that did not let anyone honestly win because Wacky Witch and Kuku Klown never had an appropriate partner.

"Nah, that's dumb."

"What about hop-scotch?" I began outlining squares on the hard-packed earth.

Cricket commenced to shuffle his feet through my gravel art destroying the careful designs.

"You twerp!" I screamed employing my best child-management skills.

Cricket took off like a bullet, I in close pursuit. "I'm 'sposed to take care of you! You have to do what I say."

Cricket giggled at this new game. He was little and lithe and could scoot behind boxes and barrels, under the orange trees, over the corral gate, through the barn, and into the back field. But, I was bigger. I could catch him. Cricket's moment of reckoning came when he took refuge in a rusted chassis that squatted in the back field. This abandoned roadster had been stripped of any serviceable parts. It had served alternately as a playhouse, a stagecoach, a fort, or a locomotive depending on the game of the day.

I pulled Cricket out of his safe harbor and began pummeling some sense into him. "I'm s'posed to take care of you! You have to do what I say."

He responded with squalls and howls.

"You'll be sorry if Mother and Daddy come home and find you dead!"

Cricket administered a swift kick that left me yowling; then he scooted off to be consoled by his dog.

My baby-sitting ego deflated, I decided to leave my charge to fend for himself.

"He'll probably be dead when Mother and Daddy get home, and I won't get paid for taking care of him." I sulked on the way back to the house.

Daddy had instructed me to take care of Cricket and to watch the house. Maybe I would still get paid if I did a good job of tending the house. I went in to the kitchen and got a drink of water. The galley was as Mother had left it. Breakfast dishes were drying in a rack on the counter. The cabinet door above was slightly ajar. I could see boxes of Cheerios and saltines, a jar of peanut butter. There were the canned staples of our diet. Tomatoes, soup, green beans, Spam, fruit cocktail. Oddments like Worcestershire Sauce and Tabasco Sauce along with ketchup and mustard. Baking soda, baking powder. Along the back of the drain board was a line of canisters – flour, sugar, lard, coffee. A bread box. A coffee can contained assorted cooking utensils – spoons, spatulas, forks, and tongs.

Plink. Plank. The faucet over the kitchen sink dripped. Mother kept a pan under the leak to capture the errant water. She would splash that water on the potted geraniums outside the kitchen door.

In a little niche between ice-box and kitchen counter Mother collected our daily garbage. We reused and recycled a good deal of what came through the house. Table scraps and bones went to the dogs. Vegetable parings went to the turkeys. The remainder of the day's detritus was captured in a brown paper grocery-store bag then carted to an incinerator behind the barn. The garbage bag generally contained soup cans and bread wrappers, Kleenex boxes and flattened toothpaste tubes, expended medicine bottles, old newspapers, and banana peels.

An oilcloth-covered table was scattered with remnants suggesting a hasty departure. Crumbs dotted the table surface. Mother had not taken time to wipe away the remains of breakfast toast. The newspaper was folded to the crossword puzzle; Mother had completed only the top corner. The *Poultryman's Journal* was open to an article on nutritional requirements for baby chicks. A half-full mug of coffee had not made it through the dishwashing process.

Muslin curtains fluttered over the windows. A couple of baskets rested on the window ledge. One contained the wooden eggs that Mother used to encourage her hens to lay if they started falling down on the job. The empty basket she carried on her daily round to retrieve fresh eggs. A milk jug was beside the door, ready to return to McElroy when we picked up another gallon of milk.

The clapboard walls were decorated with framed calendar prints. Over the table hung two samplers Mother had stitched as a young bride:

*TO A FRIEND'S
HOUSE
THE ROAD
IS NEVER LONG*

*REMEMBRANCE
IS THE
SWEETEST FLOWER
THAT IN A
GARDEN GROWS*

They were done in tiny cross-stitch and embellished with colorful flowers and sunbonnet girls. The axioms flummoxed me. The road to any of my friends' houses was very long indeed. The second wise verse could only apply to the valiant geraniums. Our attempts at outdoor flower gardening produced withered, weed-infested foliage.

Today, I was responsible for this realm. I began to fret. "What if there is a fire? If the house burns down Mother and Daddy will be mad! I will not earn my fifty cents."

Then and there I decided to save the contents of the house from impending disaster. I started with the brown paper bag nestled between the ice-box and the kitchen counter. An upside-down Kleenex box jutted over the top. For an unexplained reason, it seemed important to remove the garbage from the endangered house and set it to its own flames. I swooped up the bag and trotted to the incinerator. The incinerator was a rusty oil-can covered by a screen so that ashes from burning garbage would not fly about. I removed the screen and placed the sack in its sooty cavity. I struck a Diamond match and held it to the bag's brim. A slow flame crept around the edge of the bag. The tissue box erupted into flames. The contents of the bag crackled and popped. I replaced the screen and returned to my task of saving The Ranch.

I raced back to the house convinced that time was of essence. In panic mode, I started with the scarred pine table. It was a small drop-leaf table just right for our four-person family. I neglected to remove the coffee mug before I began the move. The mug shifted and bumped and crashed on the floor. Three jagged pieces of crockery became islands in a spreading puddle of coffee. In several heaves (the table legs hung up on the threshold) I cleared the table of the door jamb and dragged it to a clearing a few feet from the kitchen door. I returned for the chairs. One chair at a time joined the table.

Next, I went for the culinary supplies, then for the clean dishes drying in the counter rack – four plates, a cereal bowl, two milk glasses, a cup, a cast iron skillet, a spatula, three forks, a knife, and an assortment of spoons. Out the kitchen door and back. I scurried laded with trappings of the kitchen. I grabbed the canisters on the counter – flour, sugar, coffee. Out the kitchen door and back. I grabbed the bread box. And the coffee can filled with cooking utensils. I piled the items on the kitchen table. Out the kitchen door and back. I rescued Mother's pictures from the walls. Out the kitchen door and back. We would need food. I grabbed what I could reach on the first shelf of the cupboard – Cheerios, saltines, peanut butter.

Cricket appeared on the scene.

"Help me save the house," I gasped.

"Nah," he shrugged, and helped himself to an apple.

Parts of the kitchen, I realized, could not be saved. I could not budge Butane Stove... nor the ice-box. But, I could rescue the jug of milk chilling therein. I set the milk on the table in the hot sun.

I had not even begun saving the contents of other parts of the house. The Pahlah! Armload after armload I unloaded books from the citrus crate shelves and added them to my pile of salvage. I unplugged Philco Radio and carted it to the stack. Next went the rocking chair, then the mantle clock, then the piano stool. I would need my army-cot bed that doubled as a davenport. I grabbed one end of the cot, dragged it through The Pahlah, through the kitchen, and out the door. In the process I disheveled the bedding camouflaged by a Mexican serape. Bedclothes followed me in a ragged trail.

By now my energy was flagging. Judging the stash outside the kitchen door I surmised that we should have supplies enough to set up housekeeping after the house burned down. Finally, I claimed two of my favorite books and took post at my mound of salvage. I was sitting on a kitchen chair guarding the loot when Mother and Daddy turned in the drive. The household fittings occupied the spot where they usually parked.

Daddy said they were both pleased and surprised. Pleased that I had saved the house, but, maybe, a little more surprised than pleased. Mother didn't seem to be pleased at all.

"Where is the bag of groceries?" she asked after she surveyed the disarray.

"What bag of groceries?"

"The bag that was beside the ice-box."

"The bag that was beside the ice-box." I blithered.

"Yes, the bag that was beside the ice-box."

The day before, Mother had returned from market and had not yet put all of the groceries away. The week's groceries were in the bag that I had set afire in the incinerator

I walked with Mother to the smoldering fire pit. A loaf of bread was reduced to charcoal. A box of corn flakes obliterated to ashes. A cracked jar of pickles made the furnace smell like a Coney Island stand. We retrieved cans of peaches, tomato soup, and spinach, but the labels were burned off. For the next week we had to guess what we were opening for dinner.

I never did get my fifty cents.

Chapter 37

BLACK-EYED PEAS

Another Christmas was over. The holiday cadaver was stashed in our small ice-box. For a week we ate every recipe of turkey imaginable: casseroled, creamed, minced, gravied, sandwiched, and souped. Mother ground the last bits of meat and pressed them into turkey patties. By the end of Christmas week we were turkeyed out.

And, a New Year began.

Mother struggled to maintain her Southern legacy in the rough and tumble West that she adopted. Along with her china tea pot and embroidered linens she brought a host of culinary traditions from her Alabama roots.

Corn meal, in its many forms, was part of our regular cuisine. Mother stuffed the roasting turkey with cornbread and oyster dressing. She drizzled sweet so'gum (sorghum) over cornpone to create a dessert of sorts. She served hominy grits for breakfast, and fried the leftovers for dinner.

Mother made chit'lins from pork fat and red-eye gravy from ham drippings. In general, Southern cooking was hearty, fat-laced, and cooked beyond recognition. Depending on availability from our out-west grocer, Mother dished up turnip greens, butter beans, and okra in season. Fried green tomatoes were an infrequent luxury when those large beefsteak orbs were offered in the market produce section. Mother set ambrosia and chowchow on the table as condiments. And, after

Christmas she meted out parsimonious portions of homemade muscadine jelly, a gift from a distant Dixie relative.

Mother implanted certain culinary adages that may or may not have contained an element of good sense:

"If you spill salt, throw a pinch over your left shoulder to prevent bad luck."

"You can't have your cake and eat it too."

"A watched pot never boils."

"Don't bite the hand that feeds you."

"The proof is in the pudding."

"Too many cooks spoil the broth."

In fact, after we went into the chicken business Mother added a litany of maxims about eggs and chickens:

"You can't make an omelet without breaking eggs."

"Don't put all your eggs in one basket."

"A good egg will sink in water."

"To eat a chicken foot makes you beautiful." Mother laughed when she said this one, and never pressed the point.

But, she did stick to the superstition that you should not eat chicken on New Year's Day lest, like the bird in question, you will scratch in the dirt all year for your dinner.

Instead, a week after Christmas, Mother started the New Year with a classic of Southern gastronomy – hog jowls, collard greens, and black-eyed peas. This menu was supposed to ensure good luck and prosperity for the year to come. Legend had it that hog jowls warded off evil spirits. Collard greens represented dollar bills, and black-eyed peas symbolized a pocket full of coins. Apparently, there was some penalty for NOT eating the traditional New Year's Day dinner. But I didn't believe the penalty could have been any worse than the meal itself.

Research told me that after a hog was butchered, its head was chopped up with an ax and salted down. The jowl, or cheek, was cured and kept in a cool place until New Year's Day. I didn't understand why jowls were the requisite meat for this meal. It seemed like a good ham hock or even bacon bits would have given sufficient flavor to the repast.

Nevertheless, hog jowl was the star of the menu. Maybe a

classier name would have raised its status in the culinary world. *Joue de châtré* might have had a better chance of being promoted to gourmet tables than hog jowl. Look what *escargot* did for snails and *caviar* for fish eggs.

Mother had to arrange with the butcher at Bashas' to procure a genuine hog jowl. Hog jowl was like a thick slab of bacon with extra fat and extra salt. Mother cut it into strips and fried it extracting a skillet full of sizzling grease. She then boiled collard greens within an inch of their lives. They were sautéed in the hog jowl grease and given an additional helping of salt and pepper.

Some years Mother had to substitute canned spinach for the collard greens because Bashas' did not always supply a vast array of fresh leafy vegetables. And, she might have substituted head-cheese if our grocer couldn't come up with the meal's star protein. Head-cheese (sometimes called souse meat) was a gelatinous slab laced with bits of fat rendered from unidentifiable parts of a pig's anatomy. It was disguised as a luncheon meat and lurked next to the bologna and sausages in the butcher's case.

Black-eyed peas, however, were the absolute requirement for New Year's dinner. Mother always, ALWAYS, bought a #10 can of those vile little legumes. She placed a generous dollop of fusty musty peas next to the limp mass of vegetable matter swimming on our plates like ocean algae.

In earlier times these notable peas were used strictly for feeding livestock, a practice I continued to endorse. Their association with good luck dated back to the Civil War. Vicksburg, a Southern stronghold on the Mississippi River, was under siege by the Northern Army for over forty days. Hostile troops allowed no food or supplies into town. On the brink of starvation, the people of Vicksburg resorted to eating humble cowpeas –the black-eyed variety. Thus, in deference to the courageous citizens of Vicksburg as well as the Confederate States of America, once a year, the Harrison family dined on hog jowl, collard greens, and black-eyed peas.

"But, I don't like it," I whined.

"You don't have to like it," snapped Mother. "Just eat it."

Variations on that admonishment would prove to guide me over other rough patches in life.

In spite of our faithful adherence to the New Year's ritual, I had occasion to question the soundness of the practice. A coyote got into the chicken pen and created mass mayhem and murder. A rattlesnake struck our hound. The outhouse lost its roof during a summer storm. The well went dry.

I shuddered to think what would have happened if we hadn't eaten the damn peas.

Chapter 38

CHICKEN PICKIN'

Before the sun was up, Mother slipped into a blood-smeared duster. She assembled a long pole, a length of rope, and a cleaver. Mother was out to slaughter a chicken or two for dinner.

It was best to capture the dinner fowl before the flock became active. Mother tried to go after the cockerels. They were gonna-be roosters which meant they were causing fights in the chicken coop. It was time to put one in the pot.

Before daylight Mother could actually lift the selected menu item off its perch. She grasped his feet, turned him upside down, and proceeded to the slaughtering station.

If she missed the crack of dawn, the capturing process was livelier. She employed a chicken-catching rod, which was a broomstick with a hook on the end. The hook was big enough to slip around his hoary leg, but small enough that his claws and talon would not slip through. This caused commotion in the coop. The captured bird was taken screeching and flapping to meet his fate.

Mother wrapped a slip knot around both of his feet. She hung him from the top bar of the corral. With a sharp knife she pierced the arteries on both sides of his neck. The victim released his last burst of energy and squawked and flapped until he came to rest.

Sometimes Mother used the stump and cleaver method of

murder. Then it was necessary to get the bird's head in the right position. Ax or cleaver was dispatched sharply, instant decapitation the result. At this point, a headless chicken ran amok until his nerves caught up with his demise. Understandably, slaughtering a chicken was a bloody endeavor.

The dinner bird hung on the corral fence while he cooled and his blood drained. With other macabre tools Mother sliced his craw and pulled his innards. The liver, the gizzard, and the heart became giblets in our gravy.

Mother dipped the headless victim in a kettle of scalding water. This loosened his plumage, and the defeathering process began. It really didn't take Mother long to dispatch a chicken. A naked and limp carcass was ready for the soup pot. The rest was relegated to the incinerator.

When we raised broilers they were ready for market in ten weeks. At five-week intervals we had a flock ready to be picked up by a broker who carted away 500 fowl in cages stacked high in his stake-bed truck. The chickens were processed and distributed to grocery stores and restaurants around Arizona. The prime size of the fowl, as well as economics, played an important role in raising the chicks to the ten-week mark. If we kept the chicks longer we lost money because we fed them longer. They also became a little bigger and world-worn. They were beyond the size that eateries desired.

A crisis occurred when a block of truck drivers went on strike. Why would this affect a little chicken ranch in central Arizona? The company that routinely picked up our flock for market could not send a driver. Chickens could not go to slaughter. The domino effect rippled through grocers and diners across the state. Chickens were not to be had.

Mother and Daddy put on their city finery and set out to find a market for 500 chickens that had to be discharged within the week. They came home in high spirits. Small markets and restaurants placed orders enough that the entire flock was sold. . . on condition that they were dressed (properly deplumed and gutted) and ready for cooking.

Along with their high spirits, Mother and Daddy brought

home a torturous contraption. It was a metal box three feet square. Rotating inside the box was a steel barrel punctuated with rubber fingers. It was a chicken picker.

Mother and Daddy had agreed to provide the markets with fresh fowl. They were obligated to kill, pluck, and deliver the merchandise the next day. Thus began an all-night marathon. The slaughter process theretofore involving one or two unruly roosters was magnified 500 times.

Mother and Daddy took off after the first designees. And a row of twenty headless chickens flapped along the corral fence. The chicken picker was set up on a work bench under the laundry shed. A washtub of water simmered over a wood fire.

Decapitate the bird; hang him to bleed; pull his innards; dip him in scalding water; and run him through the chicken picker. It was a process. Mother and Daddy fumbled a bit at first, but they reasoned that they would get faster in time.

The chicken picker worked on the principal of revolution and suction. As the plucking drum spun, its rubber fingers grabbed the feathers and pulled them off. Loose feathers fell down the side of the drum and onto the ground so as not to cause congestion.

By midnight, The Ranch was a site of chaos, bloodshed, and flying feathers. Mother and Daddy toiled through the wee hours of the morning. Knives became dull. Water became cold. Energy waned.

Mother's hand caught in the whirling drum. She couldn't distinguish her blood from that of her victims. She acknowledged the power of a few serious blasphemies over her customary "Oh, Deahs!" or "My Goodnesses!"

The chicken picker became sluggish. It clogged. It had to be cleaned. It clogged again. It removed only the most rudimentary feathers. Resistant pin feathers were left to be plucked by hand.

Mother and Daddy got slower. And slower.

As the first rays of dawn lit the eastern horizon the chicken picker groaned to yet another halt. Daddy, with expletives far fierier than Mother's, slammed a naked bird to the ground. It was apparent that Harrison Enterprises would not meet its deadline. A mere fraction of the 500 promised fowl would be delivered to market.

Chapter 39

BOX 7, BLACK CANYON STAGE ROUTE, RFD

"Mornin' Miz Harrison. You got a letter from yer ma in Alabama." Hank, the RFD carrier, thumbed through the missives in his hand.

He held an envelope up to the light. "And, the 'lectric bill. Tsk, tsk. All 'lectric bills is up this month!"

"And, o' course, here's *The Republic*. Headlines is about them space aliens that landed in Roswell. If ya ask me our guv'ment boys better be ready for a total invasion." Hank parceled out the daily mail piece by piece to a running commentary.

"See ya t'morry." Hank waved merrily and put his battle-scarred pickup into gear. A cloud of dust billowed as he wended his way north along the Black Canyon Stage Route.

"Hank knows our business before we do," Mother snorted.

Our address, Box 7, Black Canyon Stage Route, harkened to days of stage coaches, cowboys, and Indians. Hank bounced along the very trail used by Concord Coaches that carried passengers as well as U.S. Mail sacks between Phoenix and Prescott. In times past, the trip took three rough and dangerous days. Passengers would bunk over night at points along the way – Mayer, New River, or Black Canyon City.

The postal mantra, "Neither snow nor rain nor heat nor gloom of night stays these couriers from the swift completion of their appointed rounds," encompassed not only weather conditions along the Black Canyon Stage Route, but also Indian uprisings and banditos. Yavapai and Apache Indians in central Arizona had continued to protest the invasion of white settlers until the turn of the century. Stage coaches could be unlucky victims when Indians were incited.

Also, the stage line had been the scene of many holdups. Steep, inhospitable terrain provided perfect spots for ambush. Legends abounded of stolen loot, products of stage coach heists, hidden in surrounding hills.

The Concord Stage was still delivering mail between Phoenix and Prescott when Rural Free Delivery (RFD) was launched in more civilized parts of the United States.

Now, we had a rural route carrier who left the Phoenix Post Office early every morning, except Sunday, and distributed envelopes and parcels to boxes along the Black Canyon Trail. Hank drove his own vehicle, often sitting in the middle of his bench seat, adroitly wheeling from right to left sides of the lonely road to reach boxes staggered along the route. The mail sat beside Hank in a big box. He also had a series of little cubbyholes within arm's reach. He was able to sort and arrange mail as he drove.

He carried with him an envelope full of postage stamps. Mother could purchase a few stamps from Hank, or if she was not at the mail box when Hank arrived, she could leave three pennies on top of her letter, and Hank would stamp it for her.

When Rural Free Delivery began, country folk scrapped around their farms and slapped up anything they could find to use as mail boxes – packing crates, oil drums, syrup cans. Now, people who wanted RFD service had to invest in regulation mail receptacles, tunnel-shaped boxes with signal flags that alerted the carrier to outgoing mail. Original regulation boxes were set "buggy high" within easy reach of the carrier. Now, directive height was 42 inches from the ground. Our ragged row of boxes more-or-less followed guideline standard. Box 7, the biggest and sturdiest in the row, stood at the end.

Sometimes Cricket rode Old Bill to get the mail. Other times I pedaled my bicycle the mile from The Ranch gate to the boxes. Most frequently, Mother dropped whatever she was doing and drove the truck to meet the mailman, a testimony of her loneliness and isolation in the desert.

Hank delivered yesterday's *Republic*, assorted poultry journals, and sundry envelopes that Mother dismissed as "bills." On Thursday he brought *The Saturday Evening Post* which Mother savored throughout the week. Occasionally there were precious letters from relatives afar.

> **Dear Elsie and children,**
> The sweet peas are aflame in Mrs. Devery's garden. We are reminded of when you carried a huge bouquet at your graduation. . . .

On occasion the epistle was one of sadness.

> **WESTERN UNION**
> **DEAR ONES**
> ALLIE DIED TODAY STOP VISITATION THURS NIGHT STOP FUNERAL WILL BE FRI STOP
> **LOVE MAMIE**

Western Union did not make deliveries into ranch country. When a telegram reached the Western Union Station in Phoenix it was routed to the post office and then delivered RFD the following morning.

When we had outbound communication we placed it in the post box and raised the tin flag signaling Hank to take our dispatch – a letter to Aunt Mamie, a check to the doctor, a special order to Sears and Roebuck.

On this day Mother carried a letter in her pocket. She intended to purchase a stamp from Hank and send it forth to her mama in Alabama.

> **Dear Mama,**
> I quit!
> For half a decade I have made my home at the gates of purgatory. God was in league with the devil when He created our spot on earth. He pulled every kind of thorny horny element from nature and plunked it over a sizzling sand dune. He withdrew water and set a scorching sun overhead. Then He dared His creatures to survive.

The cactus and the critters have actually done a good job of adapting to the hostile environment. Stickery prickery poisonous things, they look either angry or half-dead. For instance, the rattlesnake I found stretched beside the pump house last week looked just like a dead stick. Today a buzzard circles ominously overhead. That means he has his eye on dead meat or almost-dead meat. So far, he has not alighted. I have not identified his dinner plans.

I rescued the dog from a stand of cholla yesterday morning. He must have been rooting after a ground squirrel or a lizard, and he got too close to a plant we call the jumping cactus. One of the cactus links became firmly imbedded in his nose. The ungrateful cur bit me as I tried to pull the thorns out. He continues to paw at his nose, but I'm not going to try to help him again.

First and foremost on this forsaken ranch are the chickens. They don't belong here any more than I do. Selfish demanding creatures, they expect to be housed, fed, watered, groomed, and medicated just like truculent children. The welfare of the chickens comes before nourishing our own bodies or moistening our own lips.

It has been months and months since a drop of rain has fallen. Dust drifts against the house. It filters through cracks around the windows. It permeates the curtains. It settles over table tops. I have long since given up the notion of maintaining a clean house. After all, I can't wash a load of towels in a teacup.

The children's crayons are in a melting mode. Susan left her box of Crayolas in the kitchen window. The sun beating through the glass transformed the wax into a murky puddle. A rivulet of wax dripped from the window sill into a laundry basket full of pillow cases and white shirts.

The pump motor commences to yowl and caterwaul like tom cats in a back alley. Even the dogs hold their ears. I live in fear that our whole operation will wither and die from lack of water.

To make matters worse, Bill did not get home this weekend. His job took him to Lupton, a dusty spot in the road near the New Mexico border. He might be engineering highways across the wastelands of Arizona, but those construction feats have not reached us. Naturally, he expects me to keep the home fires burning!

He is going to be surprised to get home and find me gone! I'm coming home!

Elsie

I Wonder Why She's Mad?

When Mother reached the mailboxes she found that the mail had already come. The unstamped envelope remained in her pocket and returned to The Ranch.

When Daddy got home he convinced Mother to buy something pretty for herself.

	to SEARS ROEBUCK AND CO.		
1	Navy blue linen dress size 12	#7H469	$6.59
1	Black calfskin purse	#6B573	$4.59
1	Pair black leather pumps size 7 ½	#3S224	$3.59

As an afterthought Mother tacked onto her order.

| 1 | Man's belt, brown leather 34" | #2S587 | $2.25 |

She carried the order to the mail box and lifted the red flag.

Chapter 40

THE CHICKEN OR THE EGG?

"The chicken!"
"The egg!"
"The chicken!"
Cricket and I squabbled over the eternal question. Which came first? The chicken or the egg?
Cricket maintained that it had to be the chicken. "What do we get first? Little chicks come in big boxes!"
"What do you know?" I retaliated. "The chicks we get come out of eggs. They grow up and lay more eggs. Then more little chicks come out of the eggs!"
"If you didn't have a chicken, you wouldn't have an egg!"
"If you didn't have an egg, you wouldn't have a chicken!"
"Chicken!"
"Egg!"
"Mother!"
But, Mother could not clarify this ancient dilemma. "That's hard to say. Chickens hatch from eggs, but eggs are laid by chickens."
Even the encyclopaedia skirted the issue.
By now, I was in the fifth grade. Cricket, too, was a schoolboy, second grade. Mother had us hunched over the kitchen table copying our spelling words.

E-G-G. Cricket traced the letters three times. "I still think the chicken came first," he muttered.

The Chicken or the Egg

Daddy had changed jobs. Instead of inspecting construction projects for the Arizona Highway Department, he now supervised jobs for big highway contractors. That didn't mean he was home on The Ranch any more often. If anything, Daddy came home later on Friday nights and left earlier on Monday mornings.

I'd hear snippets of conversation.

"We need . . ."

"I'll have to take care of that next weekend, Elsie."

"Volatile market . . ."
"The cost of feed is going up."
"The price of chickens is going down."
"I can't continue . . ."
"Let's look . . ."
"We'd have to sell. . ."

Mother and Daddy began combing the classified ads for real estate. We might move from The Ranch.

Moving to a new place was much like the chicken and the egg dilemma. We needed to find a new place to live before we could move from our old place. But we needed to sell our old place before we could move into a new place.

For the next year Mother and Daddy wedged in home-hunting along with chicken-raising and road-building.

"We have to have a bit of land," said Daddy.
"Three bedrooms," said Mother.
"Closer in," said Daddy.
"Bathtub," said Mother.
"Solid construction," said Daddy.
"Dining room," said Mother.
"Irrigation," said Daddy.
"Telephone," said Mother.

We trooped through houses and estates. There were lots of nice houses. There were also lots of dumps. Specifications, details, price. Nothing fit our parameters. Months into the search, Daddy followed up on the following classified ad.

> Adobe ranch house on 2 1/2 irrigated acres. 19th Ave & Northern. 3 bdrm, 2 bath, dining rm. Citrus trees. Mature landscape. Fenced pasture. Garage. Sheds and pens for livestock. Contact . . .

"If it works out we will be fifteen miles closer to town."
"But, it's still like the country."
"You children would walk to Washington School."
"Irrigation from the Salt River Project solves the water problem," said Daddy.
"We can still have a horse!" chirped Cricket.

"A tiled bathroom," gushed Mother.
"I want the front bedroom." I piped in.
"Built-in cupboards," sighed Mother.
"Shiny oak floors."
"Thick, insulated walls."
"A fireplace."
"Fully furnished."
"Mother will get her reading chairs!"
"Daddy gets a desk."
"A four-poster bed! Just like in the movies!"
"I hope. I hope."
"Don't get your hopes up yet."

Daddy placed a corresponding ad in the *Arizona Republic*.

Rural Property north of Phoenix. 8 acres in Deer Valley. Fully outfitted for raising chickens commercially. Residence plus 10 buildings. Includes barn and horse pasture. New well on property. Contact: Box 7, Black Canyon Stage Rt.

Business on The Ranch began to wind down. Mother and Daddy had to sell off the remaining batches of chickens in their proper cycles. But, they bought no new boxes of fuzzy chicks to replace them.

Meetings and dickering occurred over both parcels of property. In a loosely orchestrated maneuver we sold The Ranch and bought the Adobe Hacienda.

Although the move was only fifteen miles (compared to 150 miles five years previously) it seemed far more complicated. For one thing, we had accumulated a lot of twaddle and tripe in the ensuing years. Also, I was older now, and expected to shoulder some of the moving responsibilities. Mother and Daddy shuttled between The Ranch and the Hacienda with numerous pickup loads of paraphernalia.

We sat among unopened boxes scattered throughout our new home.

"Well, Mother," I said, "what are you going to do after you get all this stuff put away?" Surely she would have time on her hands.

"I've been thinking," Mother mulled. "About those pens across the back fence. I believe we could bring in a few chickens..."

Author photo by Katie McMichael

Susan Harrison McMichael was born and raised in Arizona. She has worn various career hats: English teacher, librarian, business owner, paralegal, and resume writer. As a youngster Susan lived in small towns across the northern part of Arizona where her highway engineer father and her southern belle mother were part of a team that blazed roads and bridges across a burgeoning region. She was raised on the outskirts of Phoenix pre air-conditioning and pre-television. Now Susan writes homespun tales of a four-generation family that came to Arizona in territorial days and paved the way for a modern progressive state.